CHALLENGER 1
MAIN BATTLE TANK

1983–2001 (FV 4030/4 Model)

COVER IMAGE: **Challenger 1 Main Battle Tank.**

First published in October 2015

A catalogue record for this book is available from the British Library.

ISBN 978 0 85733 815 0

Library of Congress control no. 2014957454

Published by Haynes Publishing,
Sparkford, Yeovil,
Somerset BA22 7JJ, UK.
Tel: 01963 440635
Int. tel: +44 1963 440635
Website: www.haynes.co.uk

Haynes North America Inc.,
861 Lawrence Drive, Newbury Park,
California 91320, USA.

Printed in the USA by Odcombe Press LP,
1299 Bridgestone Parkway, La Vergne,
TN 37086.

Acknowledgements

My thanks are due to the following individuals, whose help has been invaluable in writing this book: Nigel Atkin (2RTR), Tim Bailey (Chertsey), Dennis Barefoot (Chertsey), Patrick Beazley (Chertsey), Andy Brend (Chertsey), Paul Burnand (ROF/RO/VDS), Olivier Carneau, Mark Cobham (REME), Andy Fisher (3RTR), Rob Griffin, Mark Helliker (Dstl), David Innes-Lumsden (QRIH), Bryn James (Chertsey), Dave Lomax (3RTR), Dennis Lunn, Robin Maclean (Scots DG), Tim Neate, Tom Packard OBE (Chertsey), Seb Pollington (2RTR), Richard Rawlins (Chertsey), David Rowlands, Michael Shackleton, Alan Sharman CBE (MOD), Brian Shrubsall OBE (Chertsey), Richard Stickland, Tony Stirling (17/21L), Harry Thompson (ROF/RO/VDS), Mike Vickery OBE (14/20H), Matthew Wedgwood, Mike Williams MBE (3RTR), Dave Wright.

CHALLENGER 1
MAIN BATTLE TANK

1983–2001 (FV 4030/4 Model)

Owners' Workshop Manual

An insight into the design, operation and maintenance of the
British Army's revolutionary Chobham-armoured Main Battle Tank

Dick Taylor

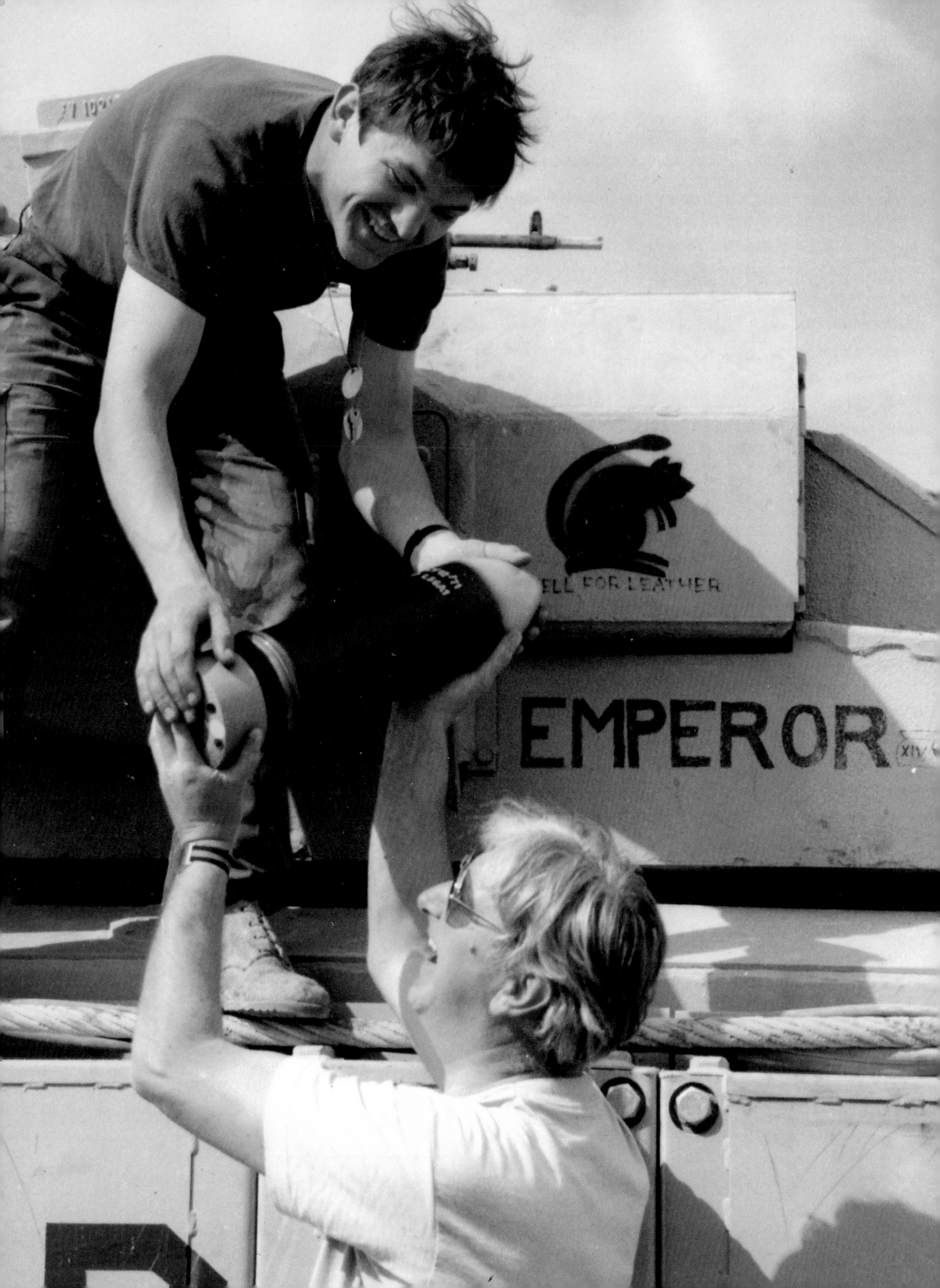
ELL FOR LEATHER
EMPEROR

Contents

OPPOSITE Bombing-up in Saudi Arabia prior to crossing the start line, Operation Desert Storm, 1991. Lt Col Mike Vickery, commanding officer of 14th/20th Hussars (14/20H) hands a HESH projectile to his gunner, Cpl Redgrave, who has the TLS key attached to the dog tag chain around his neck. The name 'Emperor' refers to the nickname of 'The Emperor's Chambermaids' gained by the regiment in 1813 during the Peninsula War. (*Courtesy Mike Vickery*)

Foreword

Major General Patrick Cordingley DSO

Until 1980 I had spent most of my military career, when with my regiment, training with Chieftain tanks. So it came as a surprise when I was posted to the Ministry of Defence's Operational Requirements Directorate to be the staff officer responsible for MBT 80, the Army's proposed new tank project.

I quickly learnt that the design process of this revolutionary tank was beset with problems. Simply put, it was proving to be too ambitious a programme and too expensive. It was the Army's equivalent to the RAF's TSR2, the advanced strike and reconnaissance aircraft cancelled due to spiralling cost in the mid-1960s. Then, in June 1980, the fateful decision was taken, on operational grounds, to scrap MBT 80. Its in-service date had slipped to the 1990s and Chieftain needed to be replaced by the mid-1980s.

I knew little about the tank that had been designed by the Military Vehicles Engineering Establishment (MVEE) for Iran. This was an evolutionary tank based on the best of the Chieftain and titled FV4030/3. Seven prototypes had been built by the time the substantial order was cancelled. And so it was, in July 1980, I was told to work with the scientists at MVEE, on the operational requirements for a tank to be introduced into the British Army that we would call 'Challenger'. For months I got home late each evening.

The turret design, with the 120mm rifled gun, progressed well, but there were too many automotive problems. The TN37 gearbox was proving to be particularly troublesome. In July 1981, the Vice-Chief of the General Staff panicked over one particularly critical report. I was sent for to persuade him not to worry. To be honest, I had no idea whether we should be concerned, and General Sir John Stanier was an intimidating man. I remember feeling very lonely sitting in his office while he told me it was my responsibility to make certain the 'damn thing' worked. Ten years later I prayed that it would as my 117 Challenger tanks waited to cross the line of departure and lead the attack into Iraq.

It was not until I joined 7th Armoured Brigade in 1989 that I actually served with Challenger and even then, as brigade commander, I travelled in a FV432 on exercises; then Saddam Hussein invaded Kuwait. I like to think 7th Armoured Brigade was sent to Saudi Arabia because we were the best, but in reality we

BELOW Brigadier (later Major General) Patrick Cordingley.

were the most available at the time and had the latest equipment of two Challenger regiments and a Warrior armoured infantry battalion. The brigade, 12,000-strong, arrived in theatre in October 1990.

Challenger had known automotive and main armament problems. We were about to find how serious these were as we learnt to fight in the heat and sand of the desert. Initially we were not overly concerned as we brought with us nearly all the Challenger engines in the British Army of the Rhine fleet as spares! During November, the power pack Meantime Distance Between Failures (MDBF) was 750km. Then, as we continued our relentless training, the MDBF started to drop to below 600km. Slack recording of engine data caused part of the problem. We were replacing engines whose history was simply not known. A 'new' engine could easily fail within a few days of being fitted. I cannot praise too highly the work of REME and the Vickers team who deployed with us, because by January 1991 the MDBF figure had risen to 1,000km; however, this was still short of the design specification of 1,200km.

On the plus side the gun was performing well and its accuracy, as far as we could test it in the desert, seemed excellent. I was thrown, however, by a completely unexpected ammunition problem. On 16 November, just as we had declared ourselves operational, the Master General of the Ordnance, General Sir Jeremy Blacker, visited me. He told me that the scientists at British Royal Armament Research and Development Establishment (RARDE), Fort Halstead, had discovered that the bag-charge used to propel the kinetic energy rounds (APFSDS) was unstable and a replacement would not be with us until January at the earliest. These bag-charges are stored in the hull in water-cooled bins to minimise the threat of an ammunition fire if the tank is hit. Or so we hoped. The general told us that if the tank was hit the unstable bag-charges would almost certainly explode and the tank would 'brew-up'.

He suggested that we re-stow all the tanks leaving gaps between each bag-charge bin.

I was in two minds. The loss of a tank crew during a live fire exercise would be tragic. On the other hand, if we stopped training to re-stow, the soldiers would want to know why and the truth would cause unnecessary concern. I decided to do nothing; but the knowledge of the danger, which I could not share, was a burden. The new charges arrived before we went into the attack.

Within days of arriving in Saudi Arabia I had decided to command the brigade from a tank. My Challenger arrived, crewed by members of the Royal Scots Dragoons Guards, and we named it 'Bazoft's Revenge', after an *Observer* newspaper journalist who was executed by the Iraqis in March 1990 for allegedly spying near Baghdad. For nearly six months I lived, worked and slept either in or near to it. It became a reliable friend. I cannot claim it was ever comfortable.

On 25 February 1991, we crossed the line of departure into Iraq leading the US 7th Corps, the largest corps in the history of warfare. It was a cold, overcast day and we were nervous because none of us had done such a thing before. But we felt confident in our tanks and this was not misplaced. Challenger was exceptional. Its firepower was devastating, with enemy tanks quite commonly being destroyed at 3,000m range. We advanced 302km in four days and destroyed some 350 Iraqi tanks and APCs. As we arrived north of Kuwait City 92 per cent of my 117 Challengers were fully fit – and that figure is remarkable.

I am proud that I lived for six months and then fought for a brief time in my Challenger 1 tank. This magnificent workshop manual has brought back many happy memories, particularly the vignettes. I always found the technical elements difficult, but here they are impressively and comprehensibly presented and illustrated.

Patrick Cordingley

Chapter One

Challenger – the 'accidental tank'

Challenger owes its existence to a series of cancelled projects, new technologies and a pressing need to replace Chieftain. Introduced as a stop-gap tank and in a hurry, Challenger went on to prove a success in combat and enjoyed the confidence and affection of its crews.

OPPOSITE A fully up-armoured Challenger 1 ready to cross the start line during Operation Desert Storm in 1991. Note all the stowage items strapped to the outside of the hull, including six boxes of composite rations stowed above the toe-armour.

9

Two generations of parentage

As with so much in the field of history, one can best make sense of the present by understanding the past – in the case of the Challenger tank a brief foray into the last few decades will help us to realise why the tank came about, and why it took the form it did. By the end of the Second World War the British Army had belatedly come to realise that the doctrine that it had insisted was correct throughout that conflict was in fact fatally flawed. Until 1945 conventional wisdom held that the army required two main types of tanks for different roles – a fast but lightly armoured Cruiser, and a slow but heavily armoured Infantry support tank. By 1944 the lack of

flexibility engendered by these artificial and rigid classifications led many to come to an inevitable conclusion – what was required was in fact one tank that could conduct the roles of both Cruiser and Infantry tank. This was referred to as the Capital or Universal tank, later to be renamed the Main Battle Tank or MBT. Certain other specialist tank variants would still be required on the battlefield, in order to overcome obstacles and to recover immobile tanks, but the MBT would be the queen of the battlefield, able to conduct both the tasks that the new armour doctrine specified, 'the destruction of enemy armour, and the close support of our own infantry'.

Britain was extremely well served for the first two decades after the Second World War by one of the most successful MBT designs ever

BELOW

Centurion Mk III.

to see service, the A41 Centurion. Proven on battlefields from Korea and India to the Golan Heights and Sinai, this design was to set the basic template for British MBTs from then until the present day. It had a crew of four: the driver was positioned offset at the right front of the hull behind a heavily armoured glacis plate of sloped frontal armour. At the rear of the hull were the engine, clutch, gearbox and final drives, along with braking and steering systems. A small auxiliary charging unit was fitted, which could be run separately to the main engine and was used for battery charging, a sensible innovation that remains to this day. Armour protection was concentrated at the frontal aspect of the hull, with correspondingly less armour on the sides, and less still at the rear, top, and belly. Mobility was achieved by the use of metal tracks, running around a series of Horstmann suspension units and pairs of roadwheels, driven by a toothed sprocket at the rear.

Between the driver's compartment and the engine compartment was what was termed the fighting compartment. Positioned above this and able to rotate ('traverse' in military parlance) all round was a heavily armoured turret in which, like the hull, the armour was distributed in proportion to the most likely area of threat. Therefore the mantlet, the external shield protecting the main gun, was the most heavily armoured part of all. Inside the turret was the breech and recoil system of this main gun, able to deliver armour defeating ammunition to knock out enemy armour, and also high-explosive shells for tackling softer targets. Two machine guns could be mounted, one alongside the main gun and the other on the commander's cupola, primarily for anti-aircraft defence. The other three crew members occupied the turret: the gun loader (who also was the radio operator) on the left in the most roomy part of the crew compartment; the commander on the right at the highest point, with the gunner forward and below him. All crewmen except the gunner had their own hatches, the gunner entering and exiting through the commander's position. Armoured hatch doors could be closed to allow the crew to fight in the most protected or 'closed-down' position. Inside, the crew compartment was a myriad of other systems, from the ammunition

for the various weapons, the intercom and radio systems, to fire extinguishers and rations. It was a cramped environment, designed more for effectiveness than comfort. The crew were trained to be, and indeed expected to be, masters of their particular trade, able not only to carry out their fighting roles but also responsible for the servicing and maintenance of 'their' tank, using the tools provided.

This basic layout and philosophy was largely retained in the next generation of MBT, the FV4201 Chieftain, the initial specification for which was written in 1954. Five prototypes were on trial in 1962, and the tank was ordered as the Centurion replacement in 1963. Entering regimental service from late 1966, 902 service Chieftain MBTs were purchased for the British Army – with over 1,100 sold abroad. The tank was an improvement on Centurion in a number of areas. It was much more heavily armoured, although, like its predecessor, it still used the tried-and-tested method of using sections of rolled and cast homogenous steel armour, welded together so that the armour also forms a skeleton or carcass on to which the other components are mounted. The glacis plate was of a novel cast design, very thick and ballistically efficient, and the driver was now positioned centrally, making his task of driving when closed down very much easier. He adopted a supine (reclined) position when driving closed down, which allowed the height of the hull to be reduced. Driving was made somewhat easier by the use of a semi-automatic gear change system. A multi-fuel compression ignition engine was used rather than the thirsty petrol engine used on Centurion, but the engine chosen was poorly designed and installed, leading to a not entirely ill-deserved reputation for inadequate availability – army speak for frequent breakdowns. This reputation was to remain with Chieftain throughout its life despite repeated and partially successful attempts to resolve the problems, ruining what was in so many other ways a fine tank for its time. An in-joke at the time suggested that the tank recognition pamphlets should be amended, to show the views of Chieftain with its gun over the engine decks, the radiators raised, and the crew in the depths of the engine interior, spanners in hands.

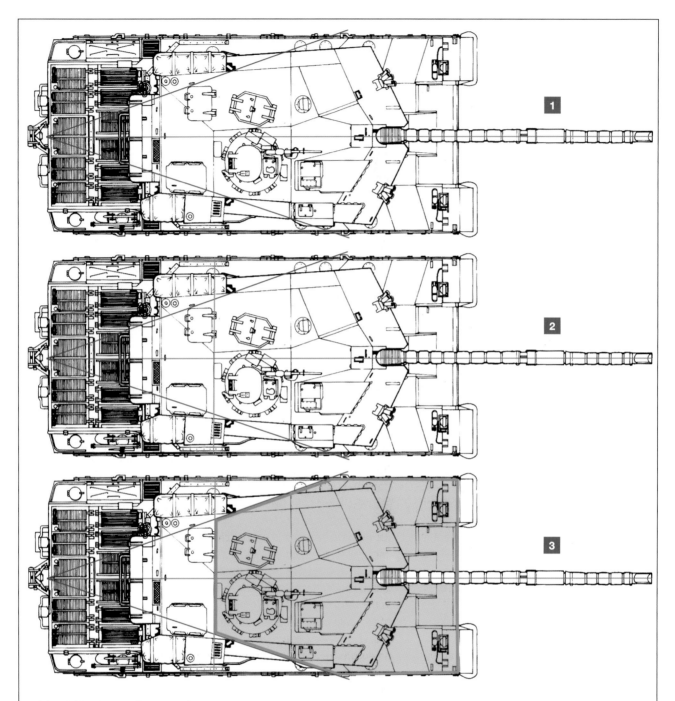

1 The Whittaker arc (aka the Whittaker Directional Probability Variation or DPV), or 'How to decide where to best position the armour on an MBT when facing a conventional enemy'. Position the tank with the gun facing front. Draw the centreline of the tank (the red line). From the rearmost point of this line on the hull draw two more lines at 30° either side (the blue lines).

2 Next, draw a line across the rear of the fighting compartment (green).

3 The area forward of the green line and within the 60° arc is the area which not only contains the crew and the ammunition but is also the area most likely to be struck by an enemy, so this is where your heaviest armour must go – the turret front and hull glacis, followed by the turret and hull front sides, on an assumption that about 66% of all hits in this area will be on the turret, and 33% on the hull. Therefore, the armour designer must take risks by using less armour in those areas outside the shaded area – the rear sides of the turret and hull, and particularly the rear, the belly, and the horizontal areas outside the arc.

The front of the turret on Chieftain was, like the hull, of a novel cast design, and did away with the heavy mantlet, putting much more armour into the frontal aspect of the turret proper. A long-barrelled rifled 120mm L11 gun, with excellent lethality and a novel system of separate ammunition, replaced the 105mm L7 gun used on the later marks of Centurion. Due to the need for ever larger calibres of tank guns, ammunition sizes had grown to the point where a single round of ammunition was very heavy and also very long, making the loader's job both difficult and tiring. Therefore, a 'Breech Loading' or BL system of separate ammunition was used, so the shell was loaded first, followed by a fully combustible propellant 'bag charge', the whole thing being ignited not by a percussion striker but by an electrically fired vent tube. This had a number of benefits – the handling of ammunition in the confined space of the turret was much easier, there were no brass cases

filling up the limited space, and probably most importantly, all the combustible components – the bag charges – could be stored in water-jacketed containers below the turret ring where, in the event of the tank being hit, the chances of a catastrophic fire and explosion were greatly reduced. Survivability was further enhanced by an engine fire warning and suppression system, and by the addition of an overpressure air filtration system, designed to allow the crew to operate in a nuclear, biological and (especially) chemical (NBC) environment, expected conditions should the Cold War turn hot.

The early marks of Chieftain were improved progressively whilst the tank was in service. The .50in ranging gun was replaced by a laser rangefinder, and then the entire fire control system was upgraded with the installation of the Improved Fire Control System or IFCS, a computer-controlled system designed mainly to enhance the ability of the tank to hit moving

ABOVE Chieftain Mk 2. Although not at all obvious from the outside, the Challenger turret internal layout would be largely based upon this design from the 1950s.

targets. This was very successful, and was followed by a turret up-armouring programme called Stillbrew, a response to increased threats posed by later generation Soviet tanks. A thermal imaging system was subsequently added as yet another 'bolt-on'. However, these were merely bandages on an ageing veteran, and the need for a replacement tank was clear. Indeed, the long development times needed with modern MBTs mean that at the moment that a new tank is introduced into service, a prudent army will be conducting two affiliated programmes: one to deliver a major mid-life improvement (MLI) package to update that tank in 10–15 years or so, and one to completely replace it in about 25 years. The initial studies for the Chieftain replacement started in 1961, two years before it was even ordered! To fully understand how Challenger came to be the tank that partially replaced Chieftain, two parallel stories must be told. One concerns the British Army and a series of troubled Chieftain-replacement projects, the other tells of the political desire and economic necessity to continue the success of Centurion by selling British MBTs abroad. We shall start with the former.

Replacing Chieftain

By the late 1960s the British Army was, quite correctly, seriously investigating the tank that would replace Chieftain. By this time the defects that bedevilled that tank were well

known, and there was a determination not to make the same mistakes again. Rather, the new tank was to have firepower that was at least as good as that of its predecessor, using a 120mm rifled gun, even better protection, and possess mobility and serviceability that the Chieftain crews could only dream of. The Military Vehicles and Engineering Establishment (MVEE) in Chertsey built a tank design called FV4211 in 1970, which basically used all the Chieftain sub-systems, including the awful L60 engine, but in a redesigned hull and brand new turret, both mounting the extremely secret Chobham armour. Much was learnt, but the project was cancelled in 1972, as hopes were to be pinned on the new Anglo-German collaboration project known as FMBT. After much discussion – and disagreement – this came to nothing and this was in turn cancelled in March 1977, leading to the initiation of a new British-only project: Main Battle Tank for the 1980s, or MBT 80 for short.

The General Staff Requirement for this, GSR 3572, was issued on 12 October 1977 and endorsed on 1 December of the same year. Demonstrating the long lead times that such projects involve, GSR 3572 derived directly from a General Staff Target (GST), an aspiration rather than a firm requirement, issued in 1971. GSR 3572 was then developed further to become the more detailed MVEE Specification 762 dated 1 December 1978. MBT 80, sometimes referred to as Project 5880, had already entered its Phase 1 Feasibility Study on

SECRET

RIGHT FV4211.

4 April 1977, and Phase 2, Project Definition, commenced on 1 July 1978.

In September 1979 the ministerial decision was made that MBT 80 would use a new diesel engine then under development by Rolls-Royce, the 1,500bhp CV12; this would be coupled to a David Brown TN38 transmission system. In order to make the best use of this step-change in engine power, a revolutionary hydrogas suspension would also be used – this had been considered for Chieftain but the technology was then too immature for it to be a serious contender. Now, however, it was a reality and would provide an unmatched ride cross-country; it was developed by MVEE in collaboration with Laser Engineering Ltd. A leap forward to overshadow even the new engine and suspension was in the area of protection: MBT 80 was to make maximum use of aluminium to save weight, and was to use a British-designed armour system called Chobham. The story of this armour is told elsewhere in this book, but the use of the word 'revolutionary' to describe it is completely appropriate. It was the biggest single advance in armour development since the tank had been invented.

The overall intention was to conduct a fairly rapid period of design and development to establish the best ways of using these new technologies, and then put the new tank in the field by no later than 1986. As it was, only two Automotive Test Rig hulls were made, known as ATR 1 and 2, the first one based on Chieftain components and made solely of aluminium, and the second based on FV4030 with an aluminium rear (for lightness) married to a steel front (for strength); ATR 2 was completed at Christchurch in June 1979 and bore the military registration 99SP27. Two turret castings were also made but were never joined to the hulls. The main armament was intended to be a 110mm gun developed at British Royal Armament Research and Development Establishment (RARDE), Fort Halstead. This was slightly offset to the left of the centreline in the turret to reduce the overall height and to give the gunner and commander more room, which was reported as resulting in the loader sitting sideways on; one RARDE report candidly stated that 'the gun was not much liked'.

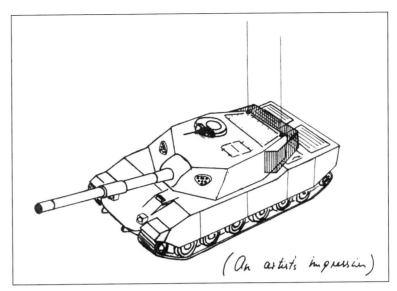

(An artist's impression)

(An Artist's Impression)

ABOVE These two images both date from 1978; the upper one may well be an artist's impression but they should have got a better artist! In British Army terms this would be called 'back of a cigarette packet' quality and is reminiscent of Sir John Carden's 1935 sketch of the A11 Matilda. The lower image is of a slightly better standard and was on the cover of a handbook entitled *Britain's New MBT*. It has the look of a cross between Chieftain and Challenger 1; in fact both are early attempts at portraying MBT 80.

However, as with all such projects, research and development costs a lot in time and money, and MBT 80 was no exception. In September 1978 the costs for development alone were estimated to be just over £127 million – enough to purchase over 100 tanks off the shelf. Many technological solutions were being explored, but the projected In-Service Date (ISD) kept creeping further and further into the future, and with no expectation that the project would be able to deliver a Chieftain replacement with an ISD before 1992 at the earliest. And horror of horrors, some influential voices were even suggesting the ultimate heresy – Britain might have to buy its next tank from abroad, with the German Leopard and the new US XM1 being the realistic contenders. Whilst all this was going on, Britain was doing good business selling tanks abroad. Centurion had proved to be a great success in both direct export sales and in after-market retrofit programmes and other development, with over £100m coming to Britain from these sources. When Chieftain was introduced into service there were good reasons to expect that the trend could continue. Israel was interested in buying the tank but was prevented from doing so for political reasons; but other countries in the Middle East were allowed to reach for their capacious cheque books and buy, buy, buy.

Foreign markets

Oman and Kuwait both bought moderate quantities of the tanks, but Iran was the largest single purchaser of Chieftain, the Shah being keen on modernising his armed forces in order to become the regional superpower. Some 707 Chieftain Mk 3 and Mk 5 gun tanks were ordered in 1971 (along with some

Armoured Recovery Vehicles and tank bridges) and these were delivered by 1976. They were largely the same as the British Army versions and suffered from the same vices. Britain was then asked to develop an updated model of Chieftain Mk 5 for Iran, known in official circles as the Project Fighting Vehicle 4030 (later it was known as Phase 1 or FV4030/1) and often called Improved Chieftain Mk 5/3P; 193 were ordered and delivered. This tank featured an automatic controller for the gearbox, a 50-gallon fuel capacity increase, better mine protection, and extra shock absorbers.

This led to a further order in December 1974 for (originally 100) 125 FV4030/2 tanks at an estimated cost of £318K per tank, generally called by the Iranian name of Shir Iran 1, Shir being the Farsi word for Lion. Shir 1 was essentially a Chieftain with its mobility massively enhanced by the use of a 1,200bhp diesel powerpack – effectively the same pack chosen for use in MBT 80 – and some suspension improvements but not hydrogas. The first three Shir 1 prototypes were completed by January 1977 and immediately started a series of trials, with MVEE issuing a revised detailed specification, No 743, in January 1979. Shir 1 was just the aperitif, though, as no fewer than 1,225 of what was to be a virtually new tank were also to be built, a massive order that was the largest placed since the Second World War and which would secure the future of tank production in the Royal Ordnance Factory (ROF) plant at Barnbow, Leeds, for many years to come.

The new tank was the FV 4030/3 or Shir 2 and the original (under) estimate of the price was a giveaway at £350k per tank – this was subsequently revised. Shir 2 was to use the new Chobham armour (sometimes called Pageant for the Iranian market) that had been announced to the world in August 1976, and which the British Army had first expected to see deployed on its MBT 80 Chieftain replacement; now it looked as if the Iranians were going to be the first to field it, even before the Americans who had been passed the technology for possible use on their XM1. It was also to employ hydrogas and be fitted with Marconi IFCS, using a Barr and Stroud laser rangefinder in conjunction with a ballistic computer to aid the gunner.

BELOW The CV12-800 engine initially specified for the Shir 1, and which ended up in service in its larger 1,200bhp version in the Challenger 1. The 800bhp version was also intended to re-engine the existing Iranian Chieftain fleet in 1981–82.

By early 1979 ROF Leeds were preparing to start mass production of both types, with additional and expensive facilities built, the assembly line tooled up, parts stockpiled, and the workforce trained, with an intention of being able to eventually produce up to 300 Shir tanks per year. No one had predicted the Iranian Islamic revolution, which erupted in 1977/78, and led to the deposing of the Shah in early 1979. On 6 February the British Ambassador was informed that four large defence contracts placed by Iran would not be honoured, including that for the Shir series of tanks, despite the fact that the Shir 1s were already in the process of being assembled, and materials and components had been stockpiled ready for the first batch of 250 Shir 2. In fact this was no real surprise; the implications of a possible cancellation were being discussed in Cabinet during late 1978; the concern was also expressed that the Israelis (and indeed the Egyptians and Syrians) might put in a 'potentially embarrassing bid' for the now redundant programme, which fortunately never transpired. India was also seriously interested in evaluating FV4030/3 at one stage, with a view to possibly buying between 300 and 1,200, and Saudi Arabia also expressed some interest. Officially at least, there was no question of the British Army being directly attracted by these tanks; the MBT 80 project was still actively in its

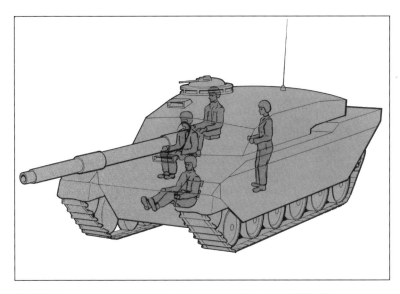

ABOVE An early sketch showing the crew positions in 4030/3. The driver is in the centre of the hull front, the loader standing on the left of the fighting compartment, with the gunner seated forward right in the turret and the commander above and to his rear. The locations remain unchanged from Chieftain, and were broadly similar to Centurion.

BELOW A prototype FV4030/3 with the nearly full-width turret and large No 84 commander's day/night sight, plus the early ribbed road wheels. Note the position of the smoke grenade dischargers and lifting eyes, nearly on the corners of the turret front; on Challenger they were to be moved inboard much closer to the main armament. This was because the turret itself had to be reduced in width to fit the European rail gauge, and also to get the right-hand set out of the sight line of the TOGS.

early project definition phase, and Shir 2 was to all intents and purposes just a variant of what the army already had, not a completely new tank with all the latest bells and whistles with which to replace Chieftain.

Fortunately, in February 1979 the Royal Jordanian Army expressed interest in buying up to 600 tanks of a modified version of Shir 1 (with IFCS, a combined day/night sight for the commander, and an improved Horstmann suspension system) to be named after the seventh-century leader Khalid ibn al Waleed – as long as a sensible price could be agreed. The deal had some stiff competition, as the USSR was offering to sell T72s at $1.3m each and the USA M60A3s at $1.2m, about two-thirds the price of the Khalid, and at least in part the decision seems to have been made by the Jordanians in expectation that the British Army would themselves be ordering the tank in the future. However, contract discussions moved on very rapidly, and on 28 November 1979 a £266m order was placed for 274 Khalid tanks at £820k per tank, plus 21 ARVs and 5 AVLBs, as well as spares and support, securing the future of the Leeds plant in the short term and solving the immediate problem. However, the unscheduled and unauthorised public announcement of the deal by Douglas

Hurd a few days later greatly annoyed the Jordanians who had asked that the deal should not be publicised. The commercial wrangles over the Iranian cancellation are still ongoing, as a significant part of the cost, around £44 million for Shir 1 and £223m for Shir 2, had been paid up front by the Shah – 'pre-funding' – but no tanks were delivered. In April 2010 an international tribunal ordered that Britain was to pay $650m to Iran; however, at the time of writing Iran is subject to international sanctions and so the money passed into a trust account containing frozen Iranian assets.

Replacing Chieftain – again

We can now return to the problem that we left the British Army with earlier: MBT 80 involved huge technological risk and was not going to be ready for years – but the replacement for the 638 Chieftains in front-line service (in West Germany) was ever more urgently required, as advances in Soviet tanks and their offensive capabilities were making it – some would argue had already made it – obsolete. Interestingly, and despite the official line, some consideration had already been given as to whether the Shir 2 design might be able to form the basis of the new British Army tank, but it was concluded that as the tank was at heart an evolution of Chieftain, the MBT 80 project was the better course of action for the long term. Shir 2, although not in production, was in an advanced state of design, the responsibility for its development being with the design authority, the government-run MVEE at Chertsey and with the design parent, ROF Leeds. Both these organisations worked closely together; for example, a team from ROF Leeds spent a couple of months at Chertsey as the wooden mock-up was developed; at the end of the process, the hull design was finalised and Leeds had the detail needed to tool up the factory for production.

Seven prototypes of Shir 2 FV4030/3 were built; in due course these were to become trials vehicles V4C1–V4C7 and used for Challenger development. This design featured a completely different hull from that on Chieftain/Shir 1, and used the favoured CV12/TN37 powerpack with the novel hydrogas suspension. The turret interior was based on the latest model Chieftain but with many improvements. Best of all, the hull and turret were well protected by Chobham armour. Due to time, money and *realpolitik* the options for the British military and government

were now limited: continue with Chieftain into the foreseeable future and start yet another new replacement programme (MBT90?); buy either Leopard or M1;[1] or bite the bullet and develop the Shir 2 into the next MBT. As early as March 1979, one month after the Iranian repudiation, a policy option to buy 250 Shir 2 'for the British Army using the material purchased for Iran' was being seriously discussed. This, of course, is what happened, the project being labelled FV4040/4. On 14 July 1980 – an amazingly short period of time in which to make such a momentous decision – the government announced that around £338m was to be made available to purchase 243 tanks (237 service plus 6 pre-production) of this new design, in order to equip the four armoured regiments in one of the armoured divisions in Germany.[2] This number was not anything like enough to replace the entire Chieftain fleet, although an option for a second buy to take the total to between 350 and 450 tanks, representing half the total tank

---

1   One source noted that some consideration was given to the possibility of buying M1 turrets and hulls and fitting them out with British powerpacks, rifled guns etc. – sensibly this came to nothing.

2   This was just the official announcement: the actual decision had been made the previous month, on 16 June.

LEFT A Shir 2 on trials, clearly revealing the wider turret armour and the stowage arrangements on the turret rear. *(Courtesy Richard Rawlins)*

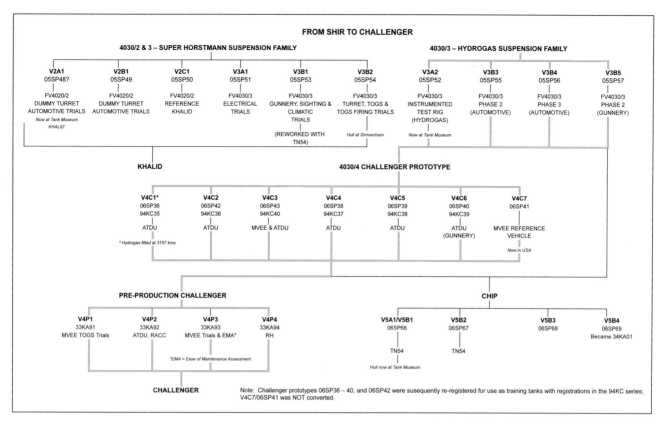

FROM SHIR TO CHALLENGER

4030/2 & 3 – SUPER HORSTMANN SUSPENSION FAMILY

V2A1 05SP48?	**V2B1** 05SP49	**V2C1** 05SP50	**V3A1** 05SP51	**V3B1** 05SP53	**V3B2** 05SP54
FV4020/2 DUMMY TURRET AUTOMOTIVE TRIALS	FV4020/2 DUMMY TURRET AUTOMOTIVE TRIALS	FV4020/2 REFERENCE KHALID	FV4030/3 ELECTRICAL TRIALS	FV4030/3 GUNNERY, SIGHTING & CLIMATIC TRIALS	FV4030/3 TURRET, TOGS & TOGS FIRING TRIALS
Now at Tank Museum KHALID'				(REWORKED WITH TN54)	*Hull at Shrivenham*

4030/3 – HYDROGAS SUSPENSION FAMILY

V3A2 05SP52	**V3B3** 05SP55	**V3B4** 05SP56	**V3B5** 05SP57
FV4030/3 INSTRUMENTED TEST RIG (HYDROGAS)	FV4030/3 PHASE 2 (AUTOMOTIVE)	FV4030/3 PHASE 3 (AUTOMOTIVE)	FV4030/3 PHASE 2 (GUNNERY)
Now at Tank Museum			

KHALID

4030/4 CHALLENGER PROTOTYPE

V4C1* 06SP36 94KC35	**V4C2** 06SP42 94KC36	**V4C3** 06SP43 94KC40	**V4C4** 06SP38 94KC37	**V4C5** 06SP39 94KC38	**V4C6** 06SP40 94KC39	**V4C7** 06SP41
ATDU	ATDU	MVEE & ATDU	ATDU	ATDU	ATDU (GUNNERY)	MVEE REFERENCE VEHICLE
* Hydrogas fitted at 3157 kms						*Now in USA*

PRE-PRODUCTION CHALLENGER

V4P1 33KA91	**V4P2** 33KA92	**V4P3** 33KA93	**V4P4** 33KA94
MVEE TOGS Trials	ATDU, RACC	MVEE Trials & EMA*	RH
		*EMA = Ease of Maintenance Assessment	

CHALLENGER

CHIP

V5A1/V5B1 06SP66	**V5B2** 06SP67	**V5B3** 06SP68	**V5B4** 06SP69
TN54	TN54		Became 34KA01
Hull now at Tank Museum			

Note: Challenger prototypes 06SP36 – 40, and 06SP42 were s1bsequently re-registered for use as training tanks with registrations in the 94KC series; V4C7/06SP41 was NOT converted.

ABOVE Shir to Challenger.

fleet, was being considered at the same time. The same announcement also officially killed off MBT 80. Although the decision to buy a new tank was thus officially announced in mid-1980, it seems that to all intents and purposes the choice had been made on 24 September 1979, with the name Challenger increasingly being associated with the project. (Indeed, by 1980 the division between what was now called Challenger 1 and a brand new tank being referred to as Challenger 2 was already being used in the upper echelons of the military.)

The tank that quickly appeared from this decision was officially named Challenger; when its replacement was introduced in the mid-1990s as Challenger 2 it was decided that, to avoid confusion, the original tank should be referred to as Challenger 1, abbreviated as CR1. The choice of name is worthy of comment: it was common knowledge that

RIGHT 06SP40 (AKA V4C6), an ATDU vehicle in a rather fetching black over green tiger-stripe camouflage, firing at Lulworth tank ranges. 06SP39, another ATDU-operated vehicle used a similar scheme.

ABOVE A top-down
view of Shir 2, and the
different rear turret
configuration is very
clearly illustrated,
as is the larger
commander's day/
night sight.

Britain had, since about 1941, named most
of its tanks starting with the letter C. In 1978
some consideration was given to naming MBT
80, with names considered, but discarded,
including Commander, Champion, Cerberus,
Chevalier, Campaigner, Corsair and Caliph – the
last two were thought to appeal to potential
Middle Eastern markets! The three main
contenders emerged as Gladiator, Lion and
Cavalier, the latter being a reuse of a Second
World War-era name. Few people knew that
the name Challenger had also already been
used, for a not-very-successful stop-gap tank
of 1944, but as only 200 had been made it
was thought that this didn't really count and
Challenger could be safely reused. At one point
it looked as if the name Cheviot was going to
be adopted, but this was dropped for unknown
reasons – probably simply that a very senior
officer decided that he did not like it. (When
Challenger 2 was coming into service a great
deal of effort was expended in trying to come
up with a new name that was both novel and
appropriate for such a weapon of war. Nothing
suitable could be agreed, so CR2, the project
name being used within Vickers, became the
name by default.) Within this work we can safely
refer to the tank simply as Challenger, or even
in its abbreviated form used by the crews,
'Chally'.

Turning Shir 2 into Challenger

This story has generated a huge amount of
debate, as to how much of the decision to
turn Shir 2 into Challenger was militarily sound
and how much of it was political, primarily
influenced by economic factors. In 1980 could
the nation that invented the weapon – with
a Conservative government led by Margaret
Thatcher – contemplate closing down its tank
production facilities, knowing that once shut
they would never reopen? Did the decision to
cancel MBT 80 come about solely because
of the military reason, the slipping in-service
date, or was the political/economic imperative
of finding work for ROF Leeds after the Khalid
order was complete the key dynamic, as
2,000 workers at ROF Leeds and Nottingham,
and 8,000 elsewhere, depended on another
order? Was it acceptable to buy a major land
weapon system from abroad? An open-minded
and thorough study completed by DGFVE

RIGHT The projectiles that made up the 120mm L11 rifled gun ammunition family and used on Chieftain. The enormous stockpile of this ammunition was a factor in deciding to 'Buy British' and develop Shir 2 into Challenger 1.

in October 1980 had concluded that buying a foreign tank would offer 'no operational, cost, or resource advantages which would outweigh the serious industrial, logistic and training penalties'. One of the less well-known factors which certainly tended to push the result in Challenger's favour was that Britain had an enormous and expensive reserve of 120mm ammunition that had been stockpiled for Chieftain in the Cold War. The future gun would, for purely economic reasons, have to be able to fire the same family of ammunition in order to make use of this ammunition. This was something that neither rival tank, both of which used either the 105mm L7 or the smoothbore 120mm Rheinmetall gun, could do, so the new tank had to use a British 120mm rifled gun.

The pros and cons of the arguments can be debated endlessly, but they cannot alter the fact that harsh realities prevailed, the decision was made and the Royal Armoured Corps (RAC) did end up with Challenger – and in the process a mixed fleet of MBTs. Like all tanks, including its commercial rivals the Leopard and the M1, the design of Challenger tries to strike a balance between the three prime characteristics of protection, firepower and mobility. Also like all tanks, it does better in some areas than in others, and we will discover these virtues and

vices throughout this book. Challenger was therefore an accidental tank in that it was never really wanted by the British Army; the decisions to turn Shir 2 into Challenger were born out of a combination of military, economic and political necessity. A RARDE report from the period took care to warn that the technology used on Challenger 'is at the early 1970s level'; a cynic might point out that as the turret shared something like 60% commonality with Chieftain, the late 1950s might be a more appropriate description.

The seven 4030/3 prototypes were used for trials as part of the rapid programme to turn Shir 2 into Challenger, with MVEE playing the leading part. One of the key points to note from this transformation was the need to turn a tank designed for operating in the deserts and mountains of Iran into one suited to the area where the British Army expected to fight in – north-west Europe and specifically Germany. It was not sufficient to simply take the Shir 2 design, rename it Challenger and call it a day. Instead, the procurement organisation issued the usual document which specified the 'why, what, how, where, how many and how often' for the tank – the General Staff Requirement. This was GSR 3574, first issued in draft on 5 September 1979 – note this date in relation to the other events related above, as it gives us a clue as to when decisions were actually made, rather than when they were publicly announced. In its preamble it stated:

SHIR 2 is a derivative of Chieftain retaining a conventional configuration and not exceeding 62 tonne. This GSR and the supporting Annexes represent performance targets for CHALLENGER and it is accepted that the design and development programme are structured to introduce the minimum of modifications to 4030/3 (SHIR 2) to meet an ISD which is of the highest priority. For acceptability for British Army service a modified version must generally perform at least as well as CHIEFTAIN MK 5 … in addition it must demonstrate significant improvements in terms of: armour protection against KE and particularly CE attack using Chobham armour; automotive agility; and availability, especially in terms of reliability and accessability [sic] of the automotive system.[3]

So there it was in a nutshell: in terms of firepower Challenger was expected to be only as good as its predecessor, but its protection was to be made better than Chieftain by the use of Chobham armour, the CV12/TN37 combination with hydrogas would enhance mobility enormously, and it was expected to be 'significantly better' in terms of availability – the experience of Chieftain in this respect was fresh in everyone's minds. Another point that is absolutely clear in this short statement is that time was of the essence, and meeting an ISD which was only three years away would be a significant challenge unless it was accepted that there should be very little 'meddling' with the Shir 2 design as it stood, although certain components of the GSR for MBT 80 were taken as an aspiration to aim for – if possible. The GSR was put together by the Assistant Director (Special Projects) at Chertsey, Julian Walker, working with a relatively junior RAC officer in the Operational Requirements branch of the MOD, Maj Patrick Cordingley (later to command 7th Armoured Brigade on Operation Granby). It was

not just a question of time – no funds had been approved to buy the army hundreds of new tanks and therefore financial approval had to be gained; some money was made available for the development phase but it was limited. An expression sometimes heard at the time was 'Challenger – warts and all'. One thing that had to be changed was to remodel the distribution of Chobham armour in the turret front and sides to raise it to the minimum level specified in the MBT 80 GSR; this took the weight up to the maximum allowable weight of 62 tonnes – the maximum weight determining how much extra Chobham could be fitted. A significant decision in 1981 was to make provision during production not only for ammunition stowage for the new APFSDS round being developed under GSR 3574, but also for the early retrofit of a thermal imaging gun sighting and surveillance system which was nearing maturity. The tank would have to meet an ISD of August 1984, when the first regiment was to be fully equipped with 57 tanks.

Referring back to the GSR for a moment, a key point to understand is the part of that document termed the 'Conditions of Usage'. These defined the environmental factors that Challenger was expected to work in, which of course had implications for the final design. The conditions to be met were that the tank was only required to operate within the geographical area of north-west Europe; in altitudes up to 1,500m above mean sea level; in climactic conditions C1, essentially meaning temperatures between –19°C and +35°C; and by day and night, in all weathers, and in an NBC environment. It is critical to acknowledge these requirements before discussing Challenger's performance and requirement for substantial modifications in Saudi Arabia in 1990, which we shall come to presently.

By mid-1981 the design was largely frozen with contracts placed for the multitude of sub-systems and components that were needed to start series production; the intention was to get the tank into the hands of field force units quickly, and assembly began in Leeds in 1982, with the first production vehicle being passed to the army in March of the following year. The first vehicle off the production line was the pre-production Mk 1 tank 33KA92 (which officially entered service on 1 February 1983, eight days

---

3   For the explanation of KE and CE, see Chapter 3 – The turret and lethality.

RIGHT The hull for a Mk 3 being fabricated on the production line at Barnbow, Leeds.

BELOW Flying mobility during trials – the hydrogas suspension allowed such manoeuvres without damaging the crew. *(Courtesy Richard Rawlins)*

before the first tank in terms of registration, 33KA91.) The story of the official handover ceremony at Leeds is worth telling. This happened six weeks later on 16 March, and was a media-driven event. After a speech by the minister responsible for defence procurement, Geoffrey Pattie MP, and another from the Chief Executive of ROF, Fred Clarke, the 'first' tank was accepted on behalf of the army by the Chief of the General Staff, General Sir John Stanier. An immaculate production standard Mk 1 Challenger 33KA96 was driven on to the parade by a crew from ROF Leeds, and ceremonially handed over to a crew from the first regiment to receive the Challenger, the Royal Hussars (RH). Unfortunately, it was all for show; the tank itself was never going to go to the regiment; it was the second of a number of vehicles that were destined for a more mundane (but nonetheless essential) career, trials work at the Military Vehicles and Engineering Establishment. Secondly, it was not even fully finished; after

the ceremony it required another month of work before formally being accepted for service on 18 April. The first real RH tank was the last of the four pre-production Mk 1s, 33KA94, taken over by the regiment at its base in Fallingbostel, Germany, on 12 April. It is worth quoting directly from one part of General Stanier's speech, as events he could not possibly forecast were to prove him very wrong. He said:

> Challenger has not been built to fight a war; it has been built to guard the peace. Challenger will stand sentinel in Europe for the remaining years of this century and indeed into the next. …

And there we shall end the background to Challenger, and pick up this story later when we review the service use of the tank – on training in Germany and Canada, on peacekeeping duties in the Balkans and during its severest test, which was not in Europe but in the deserts of Iraq.

BELOW 33KA91: The first production Challenger. *(Courtesy Andy Brend)*

Chapter Two

The hull, automotive components and mobility

The introduction of Challenger heralded a step-change in mobility, thanks to the superb hydrogas suspension that allowed full use to be made of the 1,200bhp engine. Although problems with the transmission affected reliability, Challenger still remained a fast tank with fantastic cross-country performance.

OPPOSITE The hull of Challenger 1 shared little commonality with its predecessor Chieftain. Its angular appearance was due to the Chobham armour and the powerful CV12 engine was complemented by the superb ride offered by the novel hydrogas suspension system.

In describing components in British military vehicles, the vehicle is always pictured with the turret and cupola traversed front into the central or 'gun front' position. All references are as if the describer is standing behind the vehicle and facing forwards. If the turret were to be traversed through 180° or 'gun rear', the right side of the turret would be over the left side of the hull. The detailed description is based on the Mk 2 tank with GRP charge bins and TOGS; variations from this description for the Mk 3 tank with armoured charge bins, and other modifications and improvements, including those for Operation Granby, are covered elsewhere in this book.

The hull – general description

The hull is made up of welded steel plates which form a frame or chassis on to which other components are mounted. Hollow sponsons project sideways from the top of the main hull to provide additional volume and stowage space. Internally, the hull can be divided up into three main compartments. From the front they are the driver's compartment and access hatch; the hull portion of the fighting compartment and the turret ring; and the powerpack compartment and access decks. A steel bulkhead physically separates the fighting and powerpack compartments. In the underside of the hull floor (aka belly) are a number of maintenance access plates. Chobham armour is mounted in the toe plate and the glacis front and hull sides, covered by thin steel plates known as cosmetic armour. Fuel panniers occupy the central and rear side sponsons. Suspension units, wheel mounts/hubs and final drive units are mounted on to the lower hull side plates under the sponsons. The inside of the vehicle is treated for corrosion resistance and then painted with aluminium silver paint; many bare surfaces have an insulating vinyl-covered cream foam glued to them. External horizontal surfaces are painted with two coats of gritty anti-slip paint; this also applies to the turret.

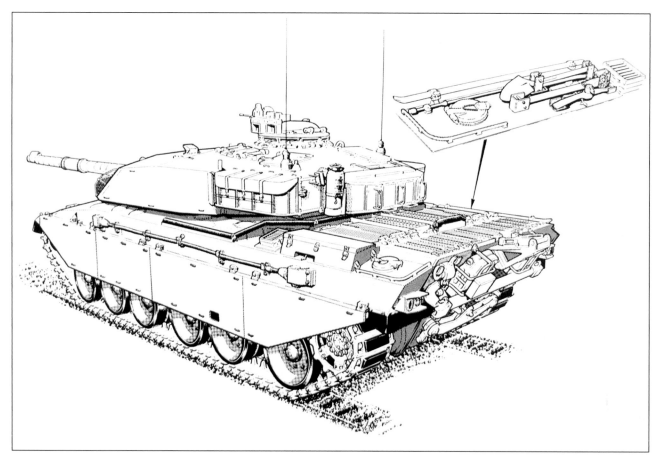

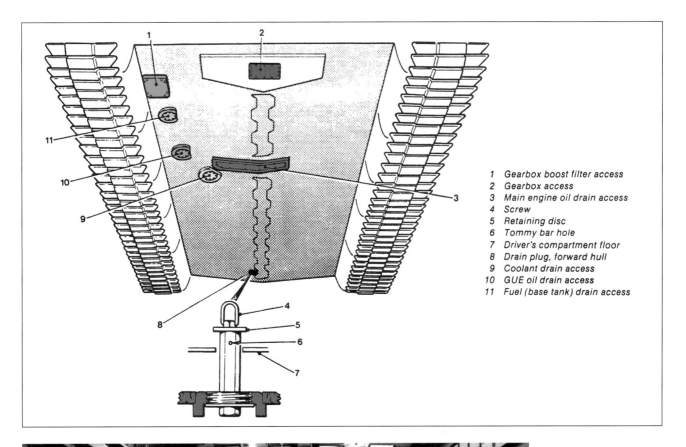

1 Gearbox boost filter access
2 Gearbox access
3 Main engine oil drain access
4 Screw
5 Retaining disc
6 Tommy bar hole
7 Driver's compartment floor
8 Drain plug, forward hull
9 Coolant drain access
10 GUE oil drain access
11 Fuel (base tank) drain access

ABOVE The belly access plates and driver's cab drain plug, from the rear.

LEFT Fitting the forward of the two rear decks during production at ROF Leeds.

CHALLENGER 1 MBT – MAIN FEATURES

1 Muzzle
2 MRS mirror and shroud
3 120mm L11 A5/A7 main armament
4 Fume extractor
5 Smoke grenade discharger (RHS)
6 Turret
7 TOGS barbette armoured door
8 MRS light source
9 Aperture for coaxial MG
10 Gunner's sight hood
11 Gunner's laser sight
12 Commander's periscope
13 Antenna
14 Spotlight
15 Cupola
16 7.62mm ammunition stowage x 3 boxes
17 Commander's periscope
18 Smoke grenade discharger (LHS)
19 Loader's periscope
20 Loader's hatch
21 Antenna
22 Camouflage net bin
23 Stowage bin
24 Driver's tool bin
25 Tow rope
26 Side skirts
27 Road wheels
28 Filler plug
29 Hub
30 Mud flap
31 650mm wide pitch cast steel track
32 Headlight
33 Hand-held fire extinguisher
34 Lifting eye
35 Towing bollard
36 Driver's periscope
37 Driver's hatch
38 Towing eye
39 Lower hull glacis (toe plate)
40 Ratchet spanner handle, track adjusting
41 Towing bollard
42 Track adjusting nut
43 Hand-held fire extinguisher
44 Horn
45 Mud flap
46 Lifting eye
47 Headlight

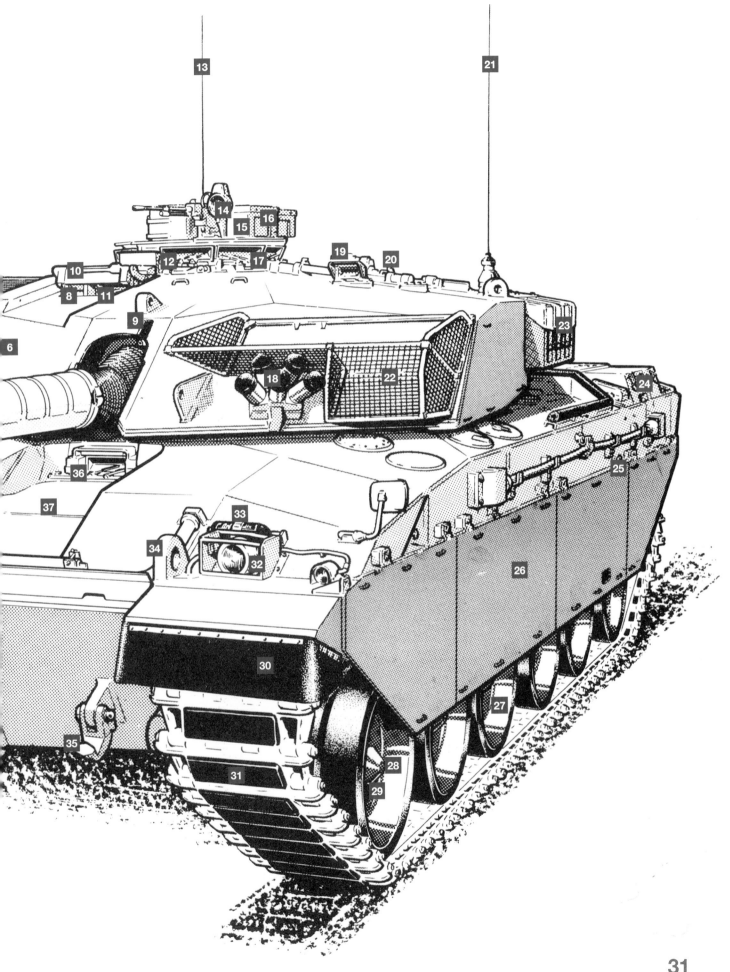

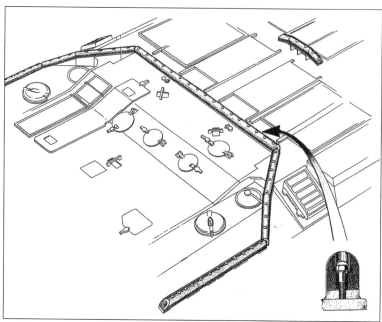

ABOVE The engine decks (aka back decks) in position. The air inlet louvres are designed to protect the vulnerable items underneath from damage from small-arms fire, shell fragments and, to some degree, chemical contamination.

ABOVE Rear deck resilient rails.

BELOW Both sets of decks lifted off a Challenger in the Gulf, 1991. Cpl Ricky Mackenzie of 4RTR (standing) is the commander, hence the 'Chinese Eyes' drawn on the front of the turret. *(Courtesy Nige Atkin)*

LEFT A QRH crewman putting the gun in the clamp: it was forbidden to do this using the powered GCE, as the dangers of a crushed hand were too great. *(Courtesy Tim Neate)*

BELOW The gun clamp, with the spring-loaded locking plunger on the base, which retains the clamp in the down position when stowed.

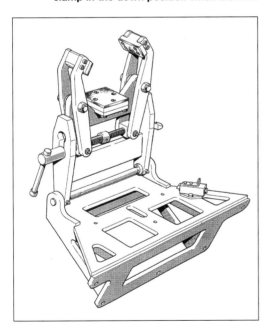

RIGHT CENTRE The full complement of recovery equipment, including the butterfly, plus jerrycans and spare track links. *(Courtesy Michael Shackleton)*

RIGHT One of the aluminium bazooka plates removed: unlike the earlier steel plates on Chieftain, these could be manhandled by one crewman.

ABOVE The first version of the exhaust louvres tended to throw any smoke (there was usually very little) straight up and therefore potentially compromising the vehicle's position, so a new sideways-facing version was retrofitted.

BELOW A close-up of the later style exhaust outlet.

EXHAUSTING WORK
Patrick Beazley

As originally designed, the exhaust from the CV12, which was always black on start-up (whereas Chieftain made mainly white smoke) was ducted upwards, only deflected slightly outwards by ballistic louvres which were little more than tread plate grilles. This was a concern because, if a tank revved-up in a hull-down firing position, its location was perfectly indicated by two four feet high black 'rabbit's ears'. I suggested deflecting or rerouting the exhaust but the engine experts snapped at this very junior engineer – 'we can't do that – it will increase the back-pressure and damage the engine – or at least affect performance'. Later, the problem remained but I had a little more authority and, even better, access to a co-operative draughtsman. I sketched out, and he drew properly, a new assembly which maintained ballistic protection, provided an increasing cross-sectional flow area as the exhaust transited out of the hull and even flattened the rabbit's ears. The engine experts of course had to point out the safety hazard (don't stand there!), but it worked and those new louvres are still there on CR2 – with a few other bits and pieces!

Driver's compartment

Numbers in brackets within the text below refer to the compartment layout diagram.

Access to the driver's compartment – always called the cab – is through a hatch located centrally in the glacis roof. The aperture is closed by a door – referred to as the driver's hatch – operated by a lever [blue] from within the compartment; it has two positions, open and closed. A retractable safety stop/plunger [yellow] is raised by a lever [red] when the hatch is open in case it should accidentally swing backwards. The hatch can be closed and locked from within [green]. A periscope is mounted immediately behind the hatch aperture. The driver has two positions: the head out or 'opened-up' position, or using the periscope with the hatch closed, known as 'closed-down'. If the hatch needs to be opened from outside in an emergency, an emergency release lug and shear pin are fitted.

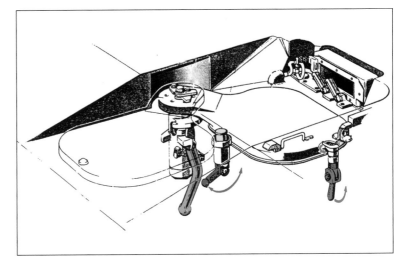

ABOVE The driver's access hatch and mechanism. The blue lever opens and closes the hatch, and the green lever locks in down against the seal to make it (hopefully) water- and chemical agent-proof. The safety stop (yellow) is raised and lowered by the red handle.

BELOW The driver's compartment – the cab – with the major components identified in the text overleaf. The seat has been omitted for clarity.

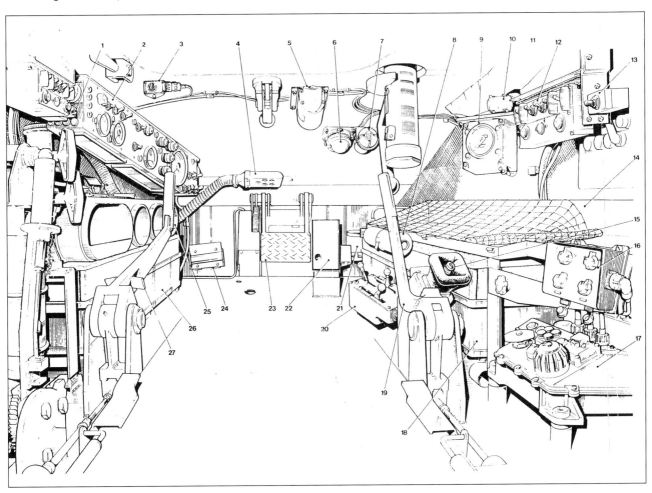

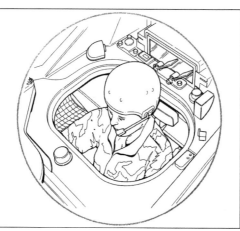

ABOVE The driver's hatch in the opened-up position.

RIGHT Driving 'opened up'.

BELOW The driver's steering levers (tillers); the bell-crank allows the driver to steer one-handed.

ABOVE Closed down. This tank has the later type of periscope cover, which enclosed the periscope completely and provided a much better seal.

With the driver sitting in his seat, his main controls are all readily to hand. Either side of the seat are the steering levers or tillers [27, 19]. These are linked and pivot around a bell-crank so that when one is pulled rearwards, the other one moves forward, and vice versa. This is to allow one-handed steering. When driving closed down, the driver raises the tillers to a more upright position.

The gear selector knob [15] is to the right of the seat within a black vinyl gaiter. Apart from neutral, there are four forward and three reverse gears; clutch operations are controlled automatically. The driver can select the following gear ranges to suit the conditions: F1, F1-2, F1-3, F1-4, R1 and R1-3. The handbrake (parking brake) is a ratchet lever to the rear of the left-hand tiller. Forward of the driver's legs are two pedals, a large centrally mounted main footbrake pedal [23], and to the right, the accelerator [22]. On the left of the footbrake is a fixed rest for the left foot [24].

On the underside of the glacis are a number of instruments and panels. The main instrument panel is located to the driver's left and forward [2]. Two smaller panels or switchboards, one for main engine starting and generation is on the right [12] and a similar one for the GUE on the left [35]. The

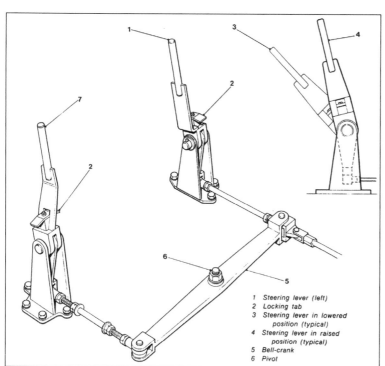

1 Steering lever (left)
2 Locking tab
3 Steering lever in lowered position (typical)
4 Steering lever in raised position (typical)
5 Bell-crank
6 Pivot

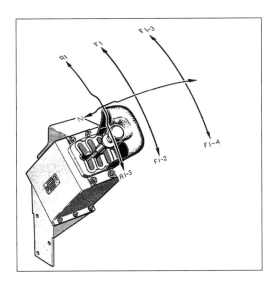

ABOVE The driver's gear selector and ranges with the vinyl gaiter cut away for clarity; the collar must be lifted up to engage reverse gears.

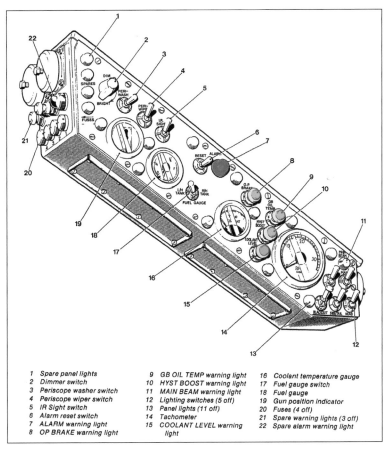

1	Spare panel lights	9	GB OIL TEMP warning light
2	Dimmer switch	10	HYST BOOST warning light
3	Periscope washer switch	11	MAIN BEAM warning light
4	Periscope wiper switch	12	Lighting switches (5 off)
5	IR Sight switch	13	Panel lights (11 off)
6	Alarm reset switch	14	Tachometer
7	ALARM warning light	15	COOLANT LEVEL warning light
8	OP BRAKE warning light		

16	Coolant temperature gauge
17	Fuel gauge switch
18	Fuel gauge
19	Gun position indicator
20	Fuses (4 off)
21	Spare warning lights (3 off)
22	Spare alarm warning light

ABOVE The main instrument panel – the speedometer is located separately to the right forward of the hatch.

BELOW The GUE switchboard, with the horn button alongside.

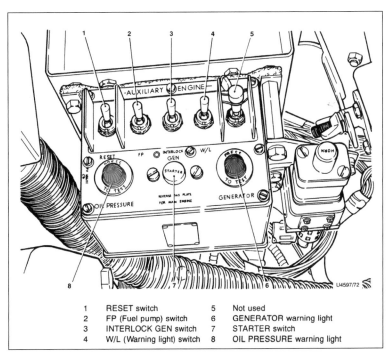

1	RESET switch	5	Not used
2	FP (Fuel pump) switch	6	GENERATOR warning light
3	INTERLOCK GEN switch	7	STARTER switch
4	W/L (Warning light) switch	8	OIL PRESSURE warning light

speedometer is mounted separately to these panels, forward right so that it can be seen readily when driving in either position [9]. Forward and slightly left of the hatch aperture is the driver's GCE safety switch [3] with two positions, safe and live, the latter allowing powered traverse and elevation to be used. A central automotive warning light [5] and a fire warning light [7] (both red) are also mounted here, as is an interior light [6].

The hull batteries are mounted in two pairs, one pair either side and slightly forward of the seat in insulated holders [26, 18]. These are lead acid types which require regular servicing, so access to them is necessary – and removing and replacing them is a heavy task in the confined space. Mounted above the left-hand bank is an ammunition rack [25] for stowing three projectiles, plus a small elliptical compartment for small items of personal kit, with a stowage position for whichever of the driver's periscopes is not fitted on the top.

Above the right battery pair is a stowage tray for rations fitted with a mesh net for keeping items in place [14]. To the left of these batteries on the floor is a box with the controls for GUE speed and fuel cut-off and the emergency gear control [20]. Finally, behind these batteries is a black box; this is the hull battery master switch box [17],

RIGHT The GUE
control box with fuel
and throttle levers,
plus the emergency
gear selector lever.

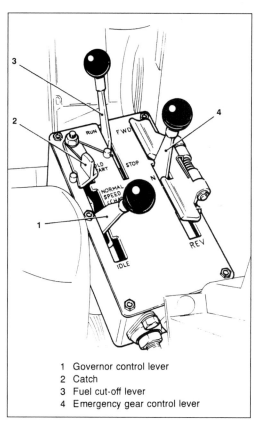

1 Governor control lever
2 Catch
3 Fuel cut-off lever
4 Emergency gear control lever

RIGHT Driver's No 36
day (right) and AV II
night vision periscopes
(bottom and far right).

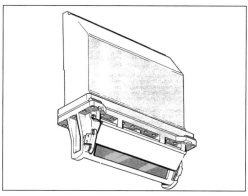

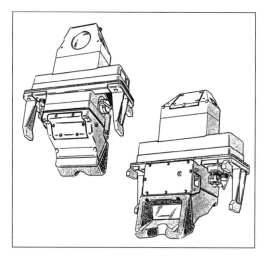

upon which is the main or master switch controlling the hull batteries, plus the inter-vehicle starting socket, used with a 'slave lead' to electrically jump start a tank with flat batteries.

The driver has two periscopes for use when driving closed down. The normal or day periscope is the No 36, a simple glass prism type, mounted from inside the tank and fitting into an external armoured cover. A wash and wipe system is provided; on early vehicles this cleans the front of the periscope directly, but on later marks the armoured cover incorporates a heated glass window and which makes for a much more efficient water seal. For night driving the No 36 is dismounted from below and replaced with the Image Intensifier (II) periscope. This receives power from a cable stowed away in a dummy socket when the No 36 is in use. The II periscope can be used in an emergency in daytime with a yellow neutral density filter selected (to prevent damage to the tube), but this is not as good as the correct day periscope.

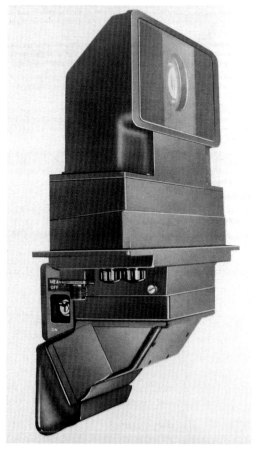

Fighting compartment (hull)

The central portion of the hull between the driver's and powerpack compartments forms, along with the inside of the turret, the fighting compartment. The rear is closed off by a steel bulkhead; the division between the rear of the driver's compartment and the front of the fighting compartment is less well defined, but is marked by two of the charge bin containers – these are covered in detail in the Survivability section. The sides of the hull walls and the top shelf of the hull sponsons are used to mount electrical equipment and for stowage, including boxes of 7.62mm ammunition. The rear bulkhead has an air inlet flap to allow the crew to select between turret and hull breathing. Normally air for the engine is drawn through the turret, as this has the effect of adding a first layer of dust filtration. However, when operating with all the hatches closed, and in particular when operating in NBC conditions, the lever must be set to draw engine air through the engine deck louvres, otherwise the crew compartment (i.e. the driver's and fighting compartments combined) will be starved of air.

Powerpack compartment

Behind the rear bulkhead of the fighting compartment is the large space which contains the powerpack (engine and transmission plus cooling), the Generating Unit Engine (GUE), plus countless associated components and systems. The powerpack ('the pack') concept is designed to increase the availability of the vehicle by packaging the engine, cooling system and transmission in one component, so rapid removal and replacement can be effected on the battlefield. Quick-release couplings and connections and a minimal need for tools assist in this. Additionally, the pack can be 'run-up' outside the vehicle on a test-bed or frame, allowing rapid fault diagnosis as well as a means of checking that a repaired pack is completely fit for service use. Another bonus for the crew is sensible design, placing those

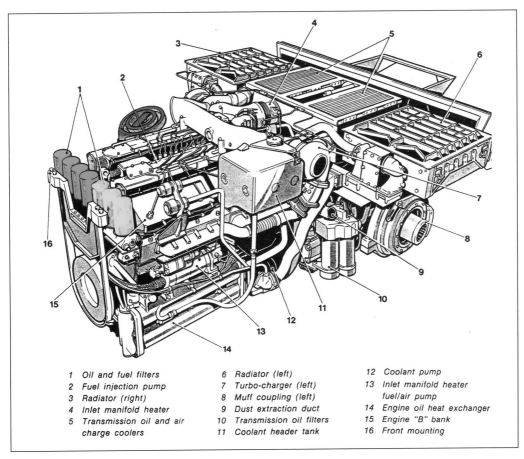

1	Oil and fuel filters	
2	Fuel injection pump	
3	Radiator (right)	
4	Inlet manifold heater	
5	Transmission oil and air charge coolers	
6	Radiator (left)	
7	Turbo-charger (left)	
8	Muff coupling (left)	
9	Dust extraction duct	
10	Transmission oil filters	
11	Coolant header tank	
12	Coolant pump	
13	Inlet manifold heater fuel/air pump	
14	Engine oil heat exchanger	
15	Engine "B" bank	
16	Front mounting	

LEFT The CV12 powerpack left-hand side, complete with cooling system and TN37 transmission.

components which need frequent checking, servicing or replacement on the top of the pack, so that the crew can access them easily and mostly without having to remove the engine decks. Oil dipsticks and fillers, filters, revolution counters, and fan belts all fall into this category.

The sky blue painted main engine (ME) is mounted in the front centre of the compartment, and behind is the transmission rigidly bolted to it. The output of the transmission, the muff couplings, are aligned with the final drive units which are mounted in the lower rear hull side

plates. Above the transmission are the radiators and the transmission air charge and oil coolers. Beneath and to the rear of the radiators and coolers are three large cooling fans. To the right of the engine is the ME air cleaner, and to the left is the GUE. The engine is a V-configuration 12-cylinder, the vee angle of 60° making the pack very compact in terms of width. The right-hand bank of 6 cylinders is the A bank, the B bank is on the left. Twin electric starter motors are employed, one for each bank. If one starter motor is defective, the engine can be started using the other one.

The brain of the operation is the main engine control unit (MECU). This is located centrally on the fighting compartment side of the bulkhead. The MECU receives inputs from the driver via his controls and from the pack, and controls fuel injection functions, vehicle speed, and the inlet manifold heater, as well as monitoring engine speed, temperatures and pressures. The ME has no mechanical controls; increasing pressure on the accelerator pedal inputs an electrical demand for more engine speed, and releasing pressure positively informs the MECU to decrease engine speed.

Fuel system

The fuel system supplies diesel fuel to the ME and the GUE. The majority of fuel, when full, is in eight connected fuel tanks

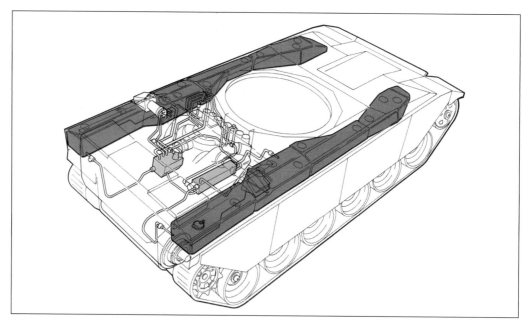

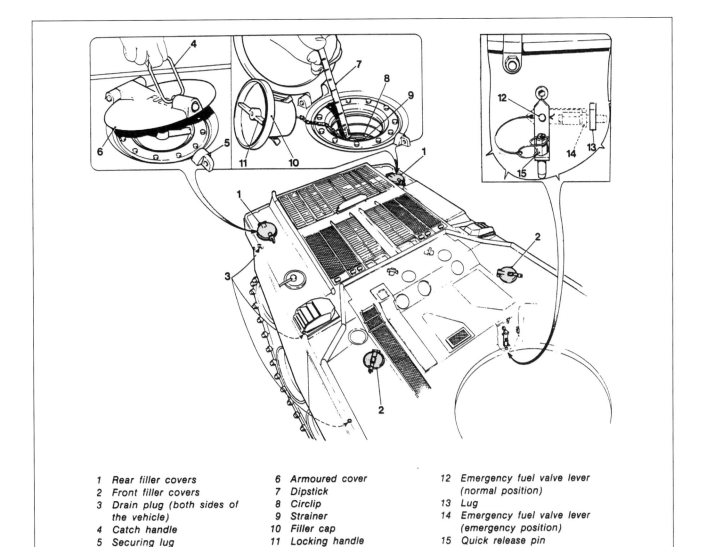

1	Rear filler covers	6	Armoured cover	12	Emergency fuel valve lever (normal position)
2	Front filler covers	7	Dipstick	13	Lug
3	Drain plug (both sides of the vehicle)	8	Circlip	14	Emergency fuel valve lever (emergency position)
4	Catch handle	9	Strainer		
5	Securing lug	10	Filler cap	15	Quick release pin
		11	Locking handle		

ABOVE Fuel tank fillers and emergency valve.

RIGHT The fuel cap cover opened ...

BELOW ... and closed.

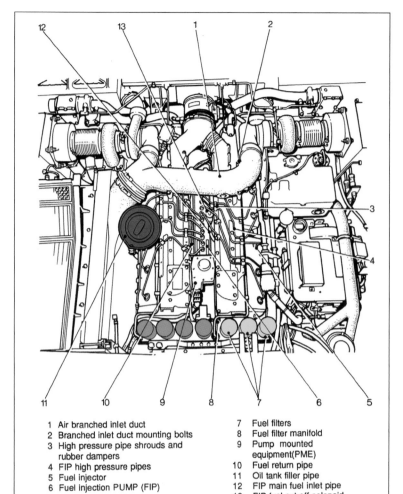

1 Air branched inlet duct	7 Fuel filters
2 Branched inlet duct mounting bolts	8 Fuel filter manifold
3 High pressure pipe shrouds and rubber dampers	9 Pump mounted equipment(PME)
4 FIP high pressure pipes	10 Fuel return pipe
5 Fuel injector	11 Oil tank filler pipe
6 Fuel injection PUMP (FIP)	12 FIP main fuel inlet pipe
	13 FIP fuel cut-off solenoid

in the hull sponsons, four either side. Each tank is lined with a fabric reinforced rubber pannier, which acts as a fuel bag, with the sponson acting as a protective outer cover. Each pannier has a drain plug, and each set of four panniers is inter-connected by distribution pipes. The panniers are topped up through four filler caps (in the rearmost pair dipsticks are fitted) on the top of the engine decks, which are protected by hinged armoured covers. A fuel gauge is mounted in the driver's instrument panel, with a switch to select either left or right tanks.

Cooling system

A system for dissipating excess heat generated by the ME, GUE and transmission is provided by two related means. The primary system is a liquid coolant-based method with two radiators, the secondary an airflow system from three fans located at the rear of the powerpack. The liquid system holds 136.5 litres of a water/coolant mix, the mix ratio and specific gravity being chosen to meet the environmental temperature conditions. The main components of the system are: a header/expansion tank mounted alongside the B bank; a pressure relief valve (PRV) and filler cap in

ABOVE The top of the CV12 showing the fuel injection 'plumbing'.

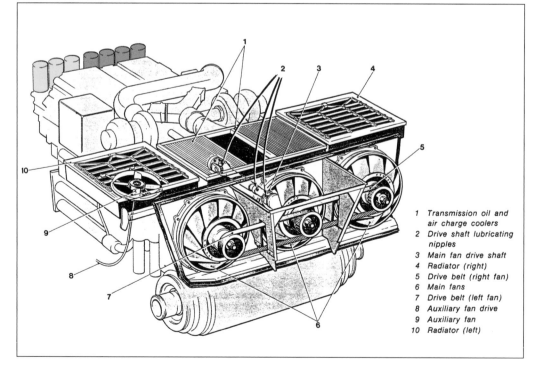

RIGHT The radiators in the lowered (operating) position, and the fan drives.

1	Transmission oil and air charge coolers
2	Drive shaft lubricating nipples
3	Main fan drive shaft
4	Radiator (right)
5	Drive belt (right fan)
6	Main fans
7	Drive belt (left fan)
8	Auxiliary fan drive
9	Auxiliary fan
10	Radiator (left)

the tank; a coolant pump in the lower left side of the ME driven by gears from the timing case; two radiators; and two heat exchangers for ME and transmission oil cooling. The driver can monitor pack temperature by the coolant gauge on the instrument panel; the maximum acceptable operating temperature is 200°F/93°C – the gauge is marked in Fahrenheit. There is also a green coolant level warning light on the instrument panel; when this illuminates the central red warning light [5] will also flash.

Gearbox, steering and brakes

The transmission makes up an integral part of the powerpack. The TN37 gearbox is rigidly bolted to the main engine, and comprises a torque convertor, a change speed pack, the hydrostatic steering unit, and the braking system. A single input receives the output power from the CV12 engine crankshaft, and two retractable muff couplings connect the gearbox output shafts to the final drives. The transmission provides automatic gear selection of four forward or three reverse gears; these are selected by the driver as gear ranges.

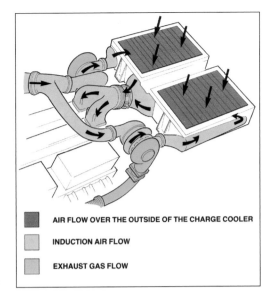

AIR FLOW OVER THE OUTSIDE OF THE CHARGE COOLER

INDUCTION AIR FLOW

EXHAUST GAS FLOW

LEFT The transmission air flow through the charge coolers, induction air flow, and the route of exhaust gases to the turbochargers.

The hydrostatic steering unit is housed inside the upper casing of the TN37; two hydraulic pumps and motors are used to vary the relative speed (and direction) of the output shafts and steering epicyclics, which in turn are transmitted to the tracks via the final drives. When the driver operates his steering tillers, a mechanical linkage and servo mechanism place demands on the steering unit and result in the tank turning to the left or the right, the turning circle relative to the gear selected. The driver can select two positions

BELOW The TN37 external; the connection to the ME output is via the large gear to the left.

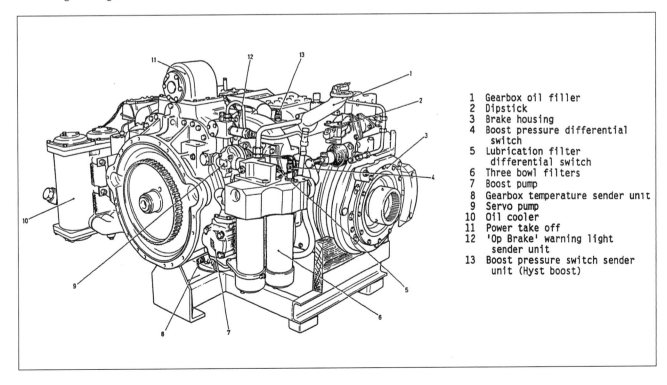

1 Gearbox oil filler
2 Dipstick
3 Brake housing
4 Boost pressure differential switch
5 Lubrication filter differential switch
6 Three bowl filters
7 Boost pump
8 Gearbox temperature sender unit
9 Servo pump
10 Oil cooler
11 Power take off
12 'Op Brake' warning light sender unit
13 Boost pressure switch sender unit (Hyst boost)

Dennis Barefoot

The Challenger 1 transmission, TN37, was in the early production phase at David Brown Gear Industries (DBGI) when I became involved with the MVEE Chertsey team who were responsible for its trials and development programme. The early objective of this programme was to demonstrate that, in a representative environment, the transmission would prove to be reliable over a distance of 2,000km. The 2,000km would comprise both road and cross-country running in cycles of 800km road and 1,200km cross-country and during each cycle there would be occasional periods of idle time to represent surveillance activities. Initially, prototype hulls (affectionately known by Chertsey trials staff as Rubber Duck, Crazy Horse, Road Runner and some with unprintable names), suitably ballasted to the projected all-up vehicle design weight, were used for the trials and the transmission would be subjected to regular maintenance, i.e. oil and filter changes, etc. Early road trialling took place on the MVEE Chertsey test track. A cycle was settled into that comprised three laps of the High Speed outer circuit followed by one lap through the Snake course. Off road running was undertaken on the Long Valley test track.

As the trials programme commenced in earnest, it soon became clear that not all was well with TN37. A serious problem with the hydrostatic steer unit pump/motor developed. The hydraulic pressure required within the unit to steer the vehicle peaked at 135 bar. This pressure led to two repeating failure types. On more than one occasion, this resulted in a vehicle running off the Longcross High Speed test track and into the stone trap bordering the circuit, spraying stones on to the roadway. This would usually end up with an irate Test Track Controller having to arrange for the track to be cleared and in some circumstances, repaired. One story that circulated about this time described how a vehicle travelling at high speed anti-clockwise round the north-eastern curve of the test track, lost steering and punched a hole in the fence that bordered the M3 Motorway before coming to rest. Quite a surprise for the travelling public, no doubt!

On other occasions, the steer unit would fail whilst the vehicle was manoeuvring out of the hangar. As vehicles emerged from the hangar, they had to undertake a neutral turn to be in a position to proceed down the access road to the test track. For a while, the risk of steer unit failure was minimised by spraying water under the vehicle tracks during neutral turns to reduce friction and consequently lower the required steering forces necessary to complete the turn. Two prime modifications were introduced into the system in an attempt to prevent further damage during trials. Firstly, an oil pressure warning light displaying on the driver's control panel would indicate impending filter blockage. This helped to some extent but it was found that the distance that the transmission would run after the warning light displayed and filter blockage occurred was very short.

A rising tide of excitement brightened the team as, for the first time, a transmission approached the magic 2,000km mixed running with nothing more than routine maintenance. As the weekend drew near, overtime for the trials team and vehicle crew was authorised. On the following Monday morning, a very glum vehicle crew was found as, despite their valiant attempt to 'push' the vehicle round the MVEE test track, all hope of completing the trial was abandoned at a distance run of 1,997km. Progressively, though, mileage increased as modifications continued to be incorporated into TN37. However, clutch pack failure, the occasional steer unit failure and random oil leaks continued to hinder reaching the required levels of reliability.

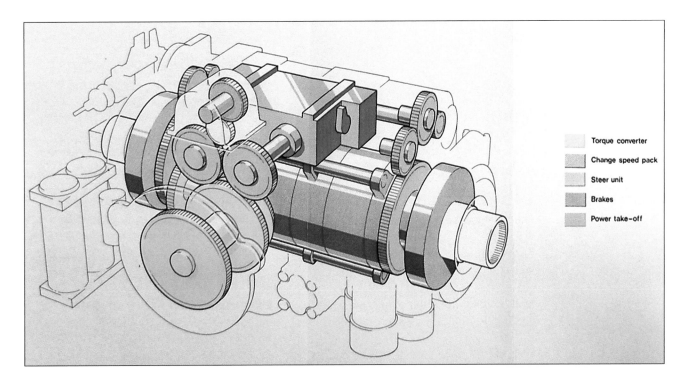

Torque converter
Change speed pack
Steer unit
Brakes
Power take–off

for the tillers – an upright position for driving closed down, and a more angled position when driving opened up. The tillers are linked behind his seat to a centrally pivoting bell crank, allowing one-handed steering. A light touch on the tiller results in a gentle turn in that direction; if a sharper turn is required more pressure is applied. When moving in reverse the opposite lever is applied, so a turn to the left requires the right tiller to be pulled – such moves are always controlled either by the commander in the turret (over the I/C system) or by a guide on the ground using hand signals. With the gearbox in neutral a stationary or 'neutral turn' can be executed as one track will rotate forwards and the other rearwards, causing the tank to turn about its axis in the direction of the tiller pulled; the engine must be revving at a minimum of 2,000rpm to achieve this.

The driver's gear selector in the cab is electrically connected to the Gear Controller Automatic (GCA) in the extreme front right of the cab. The GCA receives signals not only from the gear selector but also from the MECU, the accelerator pedal, and a road speed sensor located inside the transmission. The GCA will select the most appropriate gear for the conditions, within the range selected by the driver.

ABOVE **The main internal components of the TN37; the complexity of the unit was one of the major difficulties to be overcome in making the tank reliable, as many faults were associated with the design of this one item.**

BELOW **Steering the tank in forward, reverse and neutral turns.**

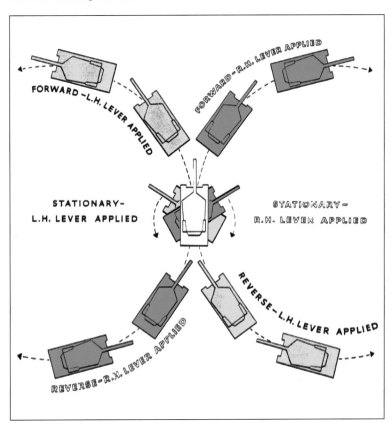

FORWARD – L.H. LEVER APPLIED

FORWARD – R.H. LEVER APPLIED

STATIONARY – L.H. LEVER APPLIED

STATIONARY – R.H. LEVER APPLIED

REVERSE – R.H. LEVER APPLIED

REVERSE – L.H. LEVER APPLIED

Final drives

Output drive from the gearbox in terms of steering and braking signals is transmitted to the track via the final drives, which have a reduction of 4.875:1. These are mounted on the extreme lower rear of each hull side plate. The final drive casings form oil reservoirs allowing constant lubrication of the gears and bearings; oil filler and drain plugs (and on later vehicles a dipstick) are provided. The muff couplings are splined in order to physically transfer the drive from the output shafts of the gearbox to the final drives. One is located on each side of the gearbox. The couplings are a slide fit, and can be easily disconnected by the crew using a special tool placed through the centre of the sprocket, thus allowing the drives to rotate free of the gearbox. This is required for powerpack removal and also to allow the vehicle to be towed.

BREAKING DOWN IS HARD TO DO

Sgt R.J. Taylor, 3rd Battalion Royal Tank Regiment (3RTR)

Towards the end of 1988 a large field training exercise (FTX) was to be held in Germany, called Iron Hammer. 3RTR were to take part, including A Squadron (A Sqn) who had finally got their quota of new Challengers and said goodbye to the last of the Chieftains. The exercise started badly for me when we in C Sqn offloaded from tank transporters and were parked almost nose to tail along the side of a fairly narrow German road. A Sqn offloaded a mile or so away and then had to drive past us to move to their first location. Unfortunately, one of the troop corporals' drivers couldn't resist the temptation to show off in his new Challenger by driving past us at speed, something that was very dangerous and which his commander should have gripped immediately. But he didn't, with the result that the right side of his tank hit mine, and shaved off all the bazooka plates and tinwork from the left of my hull, leaving me with – well, the expression incandescent with rage springs to mind. We had no choice but to pile all the now useless plates and other assorted tangled metal on to my back decks until I could

persuade the SQMS to remove them, meaning that I drove around looking the proverbial gypsies' wagon, much to my friends' delight, who knew how fastidious I was about stowage and tidiness.

A few days later I was at the head of the squadron, leading the brigade on a night march. Sod's law always states that the worst thing will happen at the worst possible time, and my (still pretty new) Challenger broke down in a narrow defile, so no one could pass me. The tank was utterly dead, engine running but no gears. We had to wait for what seemed like an eternity until the REME could come up with an ARRV and tow me out of the way, allowing the rest of the world to go past – I will never forget my squadron leader, Major David Viccars, shouting obscenities at me (he had a stammer but it disappeared when he was angry) and literally shaking his fist as he crawled past. 'It wasn't my fault Guv' might have been the politest thing that I was thinking. …

The REME were initially baffled by the problem, but eventually discovered that a large

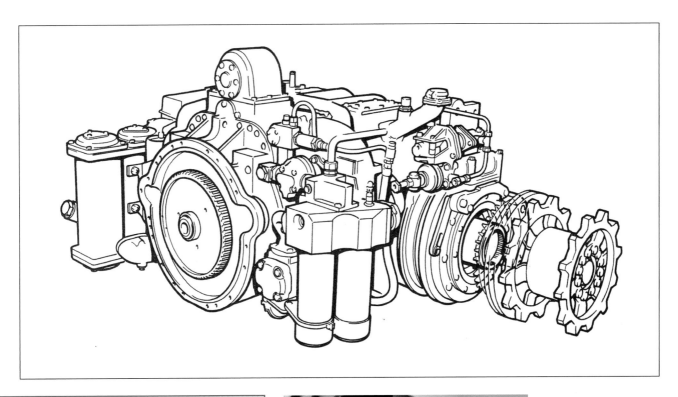

cable connected to the GCA in the extreme front right of the driver's cab – something I didn't even knew existed! – had vibrated off. Challenger suffered quite badly from vibration-induced faults; indeed, when we received brand new tanks they tended to dismantle themselves, particularly after long periods on metalled roads. The assemblers at Leeds put the tanks together correctly but didn't really 'graunch' the fittings as tightly as possible. We had already adopted the practice of tightening up every bolt, nut, clamp etc. whenever we were stopped, and also fitting spring washers wherever possible. At night on exercise the duty radio operator even had the task of tightening up everything in the turret he could get to in order to stop things simply falling apart! This was what had happened to the GCA cable, and once the cable was back on – no mean feat in the cramped space it occupies – the REME lock-wired it into position and we were mobile once again. The REME checked the rest of the tanks the following day and others were close to failing, so all were tightened and lock-wired. I never did get an apology!

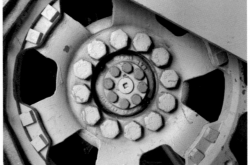

ABOVE The relationship between the transmission and the final drives/sprockets.

LEFT … And the real thing with the central end cap fitted.

The suspension and running gear

The vehicle contacts the ground by six pairs of rubber-rimmed roadwheels per side running on metal tracks fitted with hard rubber pads. Each roadwheel pair is mounted on a hub, connected to a trailing arm hydrogas unit. Drive to the tracks is by means of rear mounted toothed sprocket rings, and the track is supported at the front by a metal idler and track-adjuster wheel, and along the top by two double and one single top rollers.

The suspension units are bolted to the hull sideplate, allowing simple removal and replacement if defective or damaged; the casing of the hydrogas systems project from the rear and upwards of each mounting. Rotating

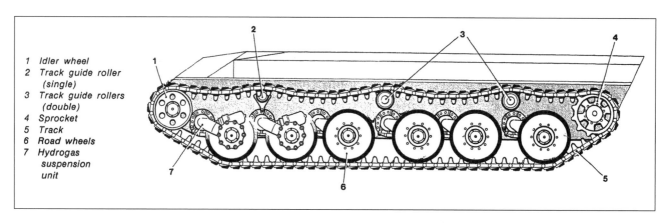

1 Idler wheel
2 Track guide roller (single)
3 Track guide rollers (double)
4 Sprocket
5 Track
6 Road wheels
7 Hydrogas suspension unit

ABOVE Components of the suspension; the right-hand side is a mirror image of this.

BELOW Suspension units and top rollers.

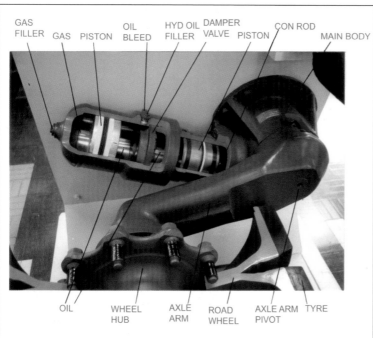

GAS FILLER   GAS   PISTON   OIL BLEED   HYD OIL FILLER   DAMPER VALVE   PISTON   CON ROD   MAIN BODY

OIL   WHEEL HUB   AXLE ARM   ROAD WHEEL   AXLE ARM PIVOT   TYRE

around the casing are axle arms with a long range of movement; on the end of each stub axle is the roadwheel hub, with ten studs for mounting the pair of wheels. In the centre of each hub is an oil filler/level plug.

The hydrogas units provide shock absorption and rebound control, giving an almost unbelievably smooth ride for the crew, and providing an excellent firing platform for shooting on the move – although the fire control system is not good enough to make best use of this. The casing houses a piston, with oil on one side and nitrogen gas on the other. When at rest these are at equilibrium. The gas pressure on the piston has the effect of pushing down on the axle arm. As the gas warms up, the gas expands and pushes down further, forcing the axle arms downwards and increasing ground clearance. When the roadwheel is moved by travelling over rough ground the axle transmits this movement to a piston operating within the housing; the piston moves up the casing, progressively compressing the gas, which increases in pressure and resists the piston, eventually bringing the piston to rest and thus the movement of the axle and roadwheel pair. Once the pressure within the gas side is able to overcome the pressure being exerted upon it, it reasserts in the other direction, forcing the piston backwards and taking the axle and roadwheel pair back towards the rest (start) position.

It is true to say that the hydrogas system, generally out of sight and largely out of mind behind the roadwheels and skirting plates, is one of the most innovative and useful

LEFT Components of the hydrogas system.
(Courtesy Richard Stickland)

SOME UNEXPECTED HYDROGAS PROBLEMS

L/Cpl Matt Wedgwood, Royal Army Ordnance Corps (RAOC)

I drove quite a few Challengers from the rail head or tank transporter on to the ship at Bremerhaven docks, both for the deployment to the Gulf for Operation Granby and also out to Canada for the BATUS rotations. One problem we discovered when loading ships was with the hydrogas suspension. When it was driven around the docks, off the rail flat or tank transporter, the hydrogas would warm up and the tank would rise, taking up the tension in the track. However, once the tank was in the hold and chained down to the deck, the hydrogas would cool and the tank would settle back down lower. This took all the tension out of the hold-down chains, which meant that potentially the tank could move in rough weather, crashing into the one alongside and even affecting the stability of the ship. The last thing the captain would want is one or more 70-ton tanks moving around in his hold! To stop this each tank had to be jacked up, two heavy trestles were placed under the front and rear of the hull, and the tank was then lowered down on to them and chained up. It could then be secured with all the weight resting on the trestles rather than the suspension, ensuring that the chains remained tight. The whole procedure was a lot of very hard and additional work, moving the trolley jacks and trestles in a badly lit ship's hold wasn't easy, plus quite a few ships seemed to have little or no ventilation so the air was always thick with exhaust fumes. The hold-down chains weren't exactly light either! During Operation Granby we loaded one ship with Challengers, Warriors and a lot of wheeled vehicles. It sailed at night but then unexpectedly returned the next morning as the ship's captain thought it was unstable and was about to roll over. We had to unload everything and reload it – the explanation that we heard was that someone had got the loading plan wrong, and all the Challengers had been stowed down one side of the ship and all the lighter vehicles down the other!

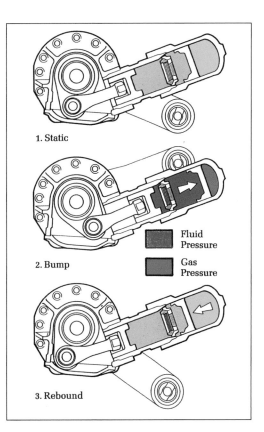

1. Static

Fluid Pressure

Gas Pressure

2. Bump

3. Rebound

LEFT The operation of the hydrogas cylinder.

enhancements to the tank, far superior to other systems used. The common torsion bar system by comparison does not offer as much roadwheel travel, and, as the torsion bars run through the hull, they take up internal volume and are difficult and time-consuming to

BELOW 79KF01, a Mk 3 tank, leans over to the left – caused more by the hydrogas suspension than the uneven ground.

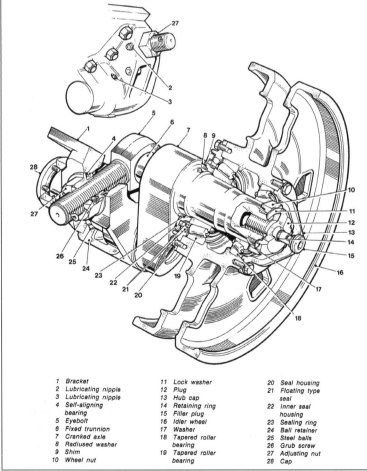

1	Bracket	11	Lock washer	20	Seal housing
2	Lubricating nipple	12	Plug	21	Floating type
3	Lubricating nipple	13	Hub cap		seal
4	Self-aligning	14	Retaining ring	22	Inner seal
	bearing	15	Filler plug		housing
5	Eyebolt	16	Idler wheel	23	Sealing ring
6	Fixed trunnion	17	Washer	24	Ball retainer
7	Cranked axle	18	Tapered roller	25	Steel balls
8	Radiused washer		bearing	26	Grub screw
9	Shim	19	Tapered roller	27	Adjusting nut
10	Wheel nut		bearing	28	Cap

ABOVE Vertical obstacle climbing in Egypt, 1985.

LEFT The make-up of the idler wheel, with the track adjustment nut and screw shown as 27. The eccentric mechanism to move the wheel forward, thereby tightening the track, is at 7.

BELOW The roadwheel, nut and washer. The combined oil level and filler plug is the same design used on the idler wheel, with oil poured in slowly until the trough is full.

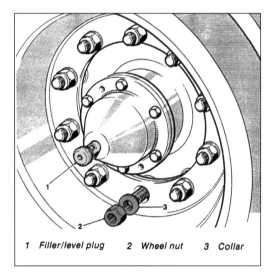

1	Filler/level plug	2	Wheel nut	3	Collar

replace. One of the few problems encountered with hydrogas in the early days was leakage of the nitrogen through defective seals. This was solved with a redesign of the seals. A 'funny' that occurred with such systems is that when they were cold, the tank settled back down on the suspension in a random way, so that at the start of each working day the tanks would be seen in the hangars in various angles of roll and pitch, often with the glacis so low as to be nearly touching the ground (and making climbing on the tanks much easier!)

A new track consists of 92 links, and can be expected to have a life of around 1,200km. Each link is joined to the next, front and rear, by a track pin which is held in place by a circlip at either end. The links have central guide horns on the inner face which ensure that the track remains correctly positioned by running between the inner and outer roadwheels, top rollers and idler wheel. A rubber pad is normally fitted to help prevent damage to roads; this is held in place by two bolts and is designed to be removable to increase traction when operating off-road. This is the theory; in the Gulf on Operation Granby this option was not taken. Slots on the outer sides of each link allow engagement with the sprocket teeth. As the track is used it stretches slightly, requiring the crew to regularly carry out track adjustment. Up to five links can be removed during the life of the track until it has to be replaced at 87 links per side. Both tracks and the sprocket rings are always replaced together.

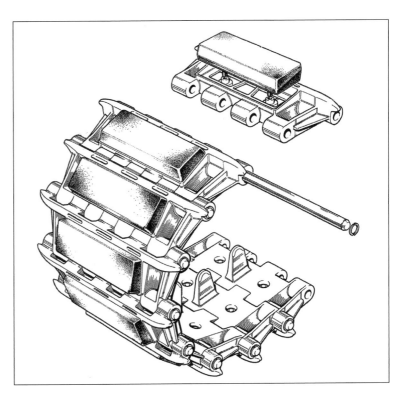

Tightening the tracks

When driving, a slack track will generally be indicated by difficulties in turning and often a loud clanking sound (meaning louder than normal). The slack in the track is measured by placing the vehicle on level ground. In order to place all the slack in the track between the idler and the sprocket, it is necessary to conduct a slight neutral turn at only 750rpm so that the tank does not actually move, pulling the steering tiller opposite to the side to be checked. As soon as all the slack

ABOVE A section of track with the track pin and circlip. The pads could in theory be removed for better traction when working entirely off-road, but this was a hugely time-consuming procedure.

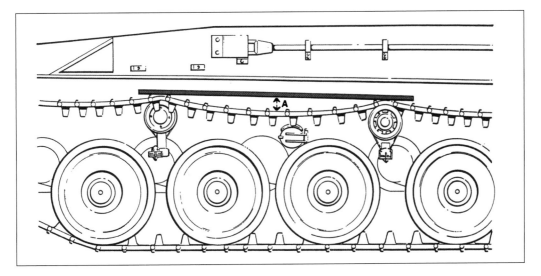

LEFT Checking track tension – most crews would do this by eye, and not actually measure the distance.

ABOVE Slack track! If a track became too slack turning would become very difficult and the danger of throwing a track was ever-present. *(Courtesy Tim Neate)*

in the track has gathered on the top run, fully apply the parking brake to lock the sprocket in that position, and then centralise the steering tillers and drop the engine revs. The amount of slack is measured between the front and centre top rollers – a straight edge may be used, but an experienced crew will do this by eye. The maximum allowable slack at Point A is:

■ Brand new track (bedding in) – 25 to 50mm
■ Bedded-in track road running – 25 to 50mm

■ Bedded-in track cross-country – 75 to 100mm

If the track is too slack, the locking plate from the track tensioner screw on that side must be removed and the track tensioning ratchet spanner – stowed on the glacis plate – placed on to the adjusting screw. The two-piece handle is then fitted to the ratchet. Two crew members can operate the handle and thus the ratchet, which will move the idler wheel forward taking up the unwanted slack. When the correct tension is achieved, the tools are removed and the locking plate replaced. When about 20 threads (100mm) of the adjusting screw are showing, the idler wheel is fully forward and a track link must be removed.

LEFT The track adjuster locking plate and adjusting nut – only about five threads are showing, so this is quite a new track, probably about 300km into its life. The plates were found to be necessary when early trials revealed that vibrations caused the adjusting nuts to shake loose on roads, thereby slackening the track.

The Generating Unit Engine/auxiliary power unit

Two types of Generating Unit Engines can be fitted, the original Coventry Climax H30 No 4 Mk 18H, or the later Perkins 4.108 – both models are interchangeable by means of a modification kit, supplied with the 4.108. The Perkins diesel engine was coupled to an oil spray-cooled Plessey generator, leading to it being commonly referred to as the 'Plessey APU'. The original terminology of Generating Unit Engine (GUE, usually referred to as the Gennie/Jenny) was a carry-over from Chieftain, and the (more modern sounding) title of Auxiliary Power Unit or APU increasingly came into use during the Challenger's service. Whichever name is used, the unit is mounted in the powerpack compartment, but does not form part of the pack. The purpose of the GUE is to run a 350A generator, in order to charge the vehicle batteries, and to provide an alternative source of high-voltage power sufficient to operate the main high-demand (power hungry) equipments, including the turret GCE, without running the ME. This is particularly useful as it is quieter than the ME, extends the ME servicing interval and uses much less fuel. It

RIGHT AND BELOW **H30 GUE left-hand side.**

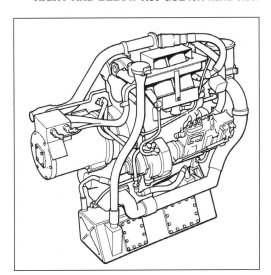

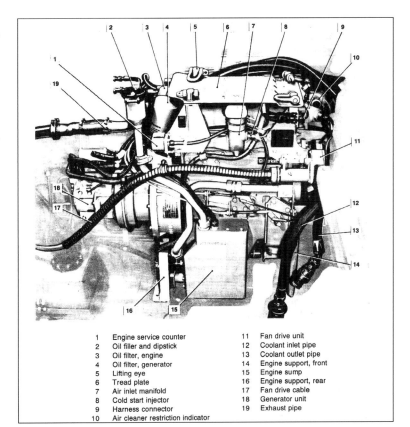

1	Engine service counter	11	Fan drive unit
2	Oil filler and dipstick	12	Coolant inlet pipe
3	Oil filter, engine	13	Coolant outlet pipe
4	Oil filter, generator	14	Engine support, front
5	Lifting eye	15	Engine sump
6	Tread plate	16	Engine support, rear
7	Air inlet manifold	17	Fan drive cable
8	Cold start injector	18	Generator unit
9	Harness connector	19	Exhaust pipe
10	Air cleaner restriction indicator		

1	Generator	7	Air cleaner	12	Speed setting control
2	Exhaust pipe	8	Revolution counter	13	Fuel injection pump
3	Oil filler and dipstick	9	Oil pressure switch	14	Blower
4	Oil filter	10	Governor	15	Oil tank
5	Fuel filter	11	Stop/run control rod	16	Auxiliary fan drive
6	Thermostat housing				

also reduces the demand on the ME generator when that unit is running. The GUE engine block and associated ancillaries, including the generator, are located in the left front side of the engine on resilient mountings. The GUE is lifted out separately from the powerpack if replacement is necessary. The change from H30 to the so-called 'Plessey' APU occurred around 1990, with the 7th Regiment, the Queen's Own Hussars, being the first unit to receive Challengers off the production line fitted with the new type of 4.108 APU – tank No 345 was the first to be so fitted. The whole fleet on Operation Granby (at least officially) used the newer model, as did CRARRV and CTT.

The hull electrical system and lighting

Connections between the major electrical components are made with screened harnesses, with cable identification sleeves fitted. Circuit protection is provided by a host of fuses or circuit breakers (CB) located on the various boxes. A CB and fuse location/ identification card is provided to assist the crew in fault-finding. Power for the hull electrical systems is provided by a bank of four – two

OPPOSITE The hull batteries: these are heavy items and the stowage racks above them must be removed in order to service them. The maintenance-free batteries supplied to Operation Granby tanks as part of the desert upgrade programme were a really welcome enhancement.

pairs – of 100 Ah batteries located in the driver's cab, and connected in series parallel. These batteries are charged by the ME and/ or GUE generators when 'on line'. Whenever these batteries are being charged, the third pair of batteries located in the turret bustle is also charged. The main components of the hull electrical systems are shown below.

Exterior lighting is required to meet mandatory legislation for peacetime. Two 4in diameter sealed beam dipping headlamps are fitted at the front on the wings, with a protective frame around them. Outside of these are the sidelights, with a pair of tail lights at the rear; the sidelights have a clear lens, the tail lights red. Also at the rear, in the right-hand cluster, is a registration light; opposite this on the left-hand side is a trailer socket. A convoy light in the centre of the rear plate illuminates the black and white striped convoy plate; many units painted

BELOW The main electrical junction boxes and components in the hull (Mks 1/2).

BELOW RIGHT The Hull Battery Master Switchbox: the 'Mazzie' is the handle on the lower left marked OFF and ON. To the immediate right of it is the inspection light socket, and then the slave lead socket, both with protective caps fitted.

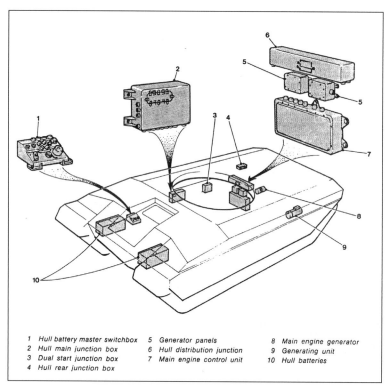

1 Hull battery master switchbox	5 Generator panels	8 Main engine generator
2 Hull main junction box	6 Hull distribution junction	9 Generating unit
3 Dual start junction box	7 Main engine control unit	10 Hull batteries
4 Hull rear junction box		

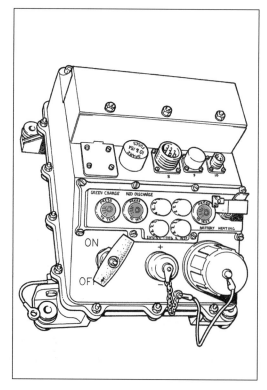

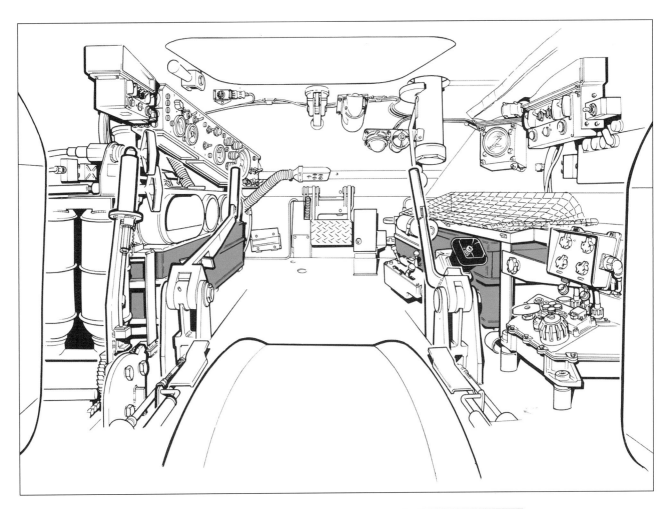

RIGHT The rear right light cluster; the registration light with its shroud to dim the light to a pinprick is on the left.

FAR RIGHT The horn – another requirement to make the tank legal on the road, although not much use when the engines are running.

the squadron tactical symbol with the vehicle callsign in black on a white square instead.

Other electrical ancillaries in the hull include: interior lights, inspection light sockets, a gun position indicator (on the instrument panel), the central alarm warning lamp and a horn – the button is next to the GUE switchboard, the horn mounted adjacent to the right headlamp.

To start the main engine from cold

BELOW The ME switchboard including starter button is to the right and coloured green; the gear selector is in red.

■ Carry out the pre-start checks (engine oil, etc.).
■ Turn on the hull battery master switch.
■ Put the ME FP and FCOS switches to the ON (down) positions; check that:

■ The Oil Pressure, Hyst Boost and Op Brake warning lights are on, and
■ The Alarm warning light flashes.
■ Put the MECU GB switch to the ON (down) position; check that the Generator warning light is on.
■ Fully depress the accelerator pedal.
■ Press the Start button, release when the engine starts.
■ Reduce pressure on the accelerator, check that the Oil Pressure, Generator warning, Hyst Boost and Op Brake warning lights are extinguished.
■ Press down on the Alarm warning light reset switch to extinguish the light.
■ Check that the IMH switch is OFF (up).
■ Allow the engine to idle for a few minutes before moving off.

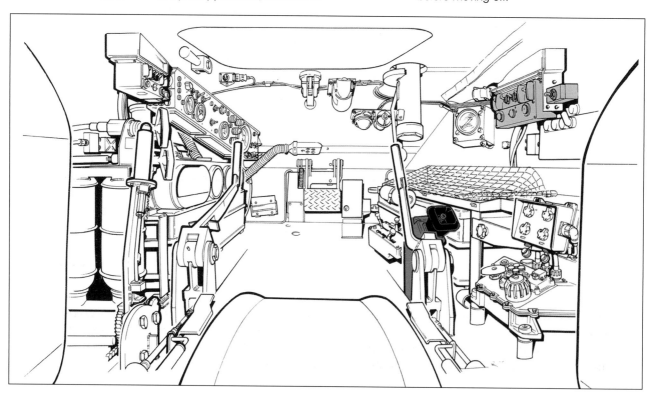

Moving off, turning and stopping

In driver training, this is the subject of an important lesson known as MOSES – moving off, stopping and elementary steering. Caution: the tank must not be moved if the Hyst Boost or Op Brake warning lights are on. If the Hyst Boost light illuminates during a turn, the turn must be immediately aborted if safe to do so, or the transmission may be irreparably damaged.

To drive off, ensure that the steering levers are in the central position. Check that the gear selector and emergency gear selector levers are in neutral. Start the engine and allow it to idle for a few minutes. With the right foot on the footbrake, release the parking brake fully by pushing in on the knob and depressing the handle to the floor. Select the gear range required: for slow manoeuvring a low range should be selected. Accelerate smoothly, avoid placing a steering demand until the engine has sufficient power; above 2,000rpm will achieve the best results. Adjust the speed and gear range to suit the terrain, using the brake to slow the vehicle and engine speed to allow the transmission to change down before manoeuvring in tight spaces or to move uphill and downhill.

A warning in the user handbook tells the crew never to exceed 37mph – just a little above the claimed maximum speed of 56km/h. (When I had a brand new Challenger in 1988 I found that we could easily cruise on decent roads at an indicated 50mph, double the speed we were used to with Chieftain!)

THE FIRST TIME I DROVE CHALLENGER

Sgt R.J. Taylor, 3RTR

3RTR became the seventh Challenger regiment in Deilinghofen in early 1988 – well nearly, as poor old A Sqn were still on Stillbrew Chieftains awaiting their Challengers to be produced at Leeds. I was a gunnery instructor and spent all my time converting crews on to TOGS, and so was unable to attend the driving and maintenance conversion myself. Within a few weeks of arrival we found ourselves on exercise on the Soltau training area; two of the tanks in my troop (10 Tp C Sqn) had been brought across with the regiment from Bovington, but one tank was brand spanking new and, as the troop sergeant, I allocated that tank to myself. Great, I thought, this will be the one and only time that I will have a factory-fresh tank, rather than the old Chieftains and even older Saladins that I had been commanding for the last five years. All we had to do was paint on the black camouflage and we were ready to go.

As the troop sergeant it is customary to have the least experienced crewmen on your tank, the idea being that the most experienced tank commander gets the youngsters in order to train them and bring them on. So when the tank suddenly and inexplicably lost all turret electrical power the other three on the tank were of little use to me in fault-finding. I applied my largely irrelevant Chieftain knowledge to the problem but could not work out what was wrong – the hull and powerpack were fine, but we had no turret power, no radios and no I/C. There were no other tanks in sight and the squadron's fitters (REME) were about 10 miles away. As we could not call for help there was nothing for it but to put the gun into the clamp and drive to them. The new problem was that I was very reluctant, for safety reasons, to let my young driver move the tank without any I/C and therefore commands from me, and in any case, this was his first time on exercise let alone on Soltau, so he had no idea where he was meant to go. I was going to have to drive it myself.

I got the driver to show me the controls, which were very simple, and as an experienced Chieftain driver I picked it up quickly. The three crewmen were in the turret with instructions to throw anything to hand at me if I needed to stop or if there was a problem, and, with my map spread over my knees, off we went. It was great! Having known the Chieftain the power and the hydrogas suspension were a delight, and although I had hated my time as a Chieftain 'cab rat', this was something else – I didn't have the responsibilities for the heavy maintenance that went with the driver's job, but was free to enjoy myself. After a few minutes I had the hang of the beast and we quickly gobbled up the miles to where the REME were located, and who soon identified and fixed the fault. All too soon it was over, and I think that apart from a few times when I jumped into a Challenger to move it short distances around the tank park or at the Gunnery School, I probably never drove one again!

To stop the main engine

- Apply the parking brake. Move the gear selector to neutral.
- Run the engine at 800rpm for up to 5 minutes to assist in engine cooling.
- Put the FP, FCOS and MECU GB switches to the OFF (up) positions. The engine will stop.
- Put the W/L switch to OFF (up).
- Turn off the hull battery master switch.

Removing a track link

Track links are removed from the rear, from the section of track between the sprocket and the rearmost roadwheel. To do this the idler wheel first needs to be repositioned – as far rearwards as it will go. This is done by the reverse procedure of tightening the track: remove the locking plate, and using the ratchet spanner in the other direction, slacken off on the nut a little. Pulling a gentle neutral turn at 750rpm will cause the weight of the track to move rearwards and thus retract the idler back; the handbook informs the crew to repeat this procedure gradually, about three threads at a time, so taking about seven goes before the idler is fully at the rear. Most crewmen would take a shortcut and instead unscrew the nut completely until it was at the very forward end of the threads, and then execute one neutral turn, which would slam

the idler back into its rearmost position and leave all the slack in the track at the rear. A practice that some people thought clever but was really dangerous, was to undo the nut fully and take the opportunity to pack the exposed threads and inside mechanism of the idler with grease by hand, thinking this was somehow better than lubricating it using the Oddy gun. This was exceptionally dangerous – should the weight of the track suddenly pull back on the idler, there was nothing to stop it retracting at speed and amputating or trapping the crewman's fingers inside the mechanism.

Once the slack is at the back, and the handbrake applied, one link can be removed by hammering on the outside of each of its two track pins with a sledgehammer to spring off the retaining circlips – considerable force is needed to do this. A circlip removing tool was provided and was sometimes used, depending on the crewman's strength and preference. Once the circlips are off, the two pins can be easily knocked through using a sledge and the 'hockey stick' punch tool. With the link removed, the two sections of track can be rejoined with the aid of a crowbar to lever them into alignment, and a new track pin hammered through to join them. All that remains is to fit a new circlip, again using a special tool, on to this pin, and then adjust the track tension as detailed above. A good crew could do this in ten minutes from start to finish.

BELOW The position for breaking the track in order to remove a link, and to connect up a new track. The crowbar (green) is necessary to push the two ends of the track together.

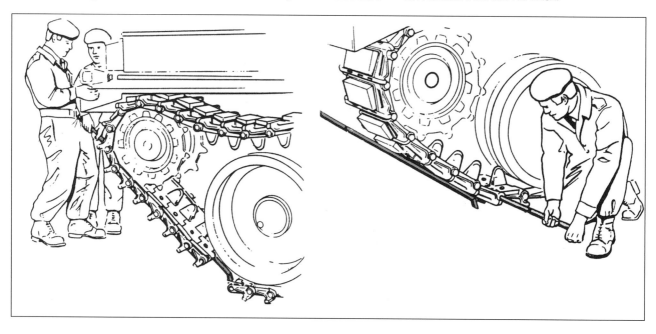

LEFT SSgt Tony Rickard of 2RTR track-bashing in the Gulf, 1990. New track was supplied in sections that had to be joined up to make a 92-link run of track. *(Courtesy Nige Atkin)*

BELOW Mobility! Strategic mobility is achieved by moving the tanks large distances by rail or ship; operational mobility as shown here is achieved using tank transporters (aka Heavy Equipment Transporters or HET) – loading tanks on and off these took no little skill and nerve.

Chapter Three

The turret and lethality

Although not immediately obvious, the Challenger turret was very similar to that found on a late mark of Chieftain. The big difference was the addition of Chobham armour, which gave it the distinctive angular appearance. Despite its age, Challenger's 120mm main armament performed brilliantly in the Gulf War of 1991.

OPPOSITE A Challenger with a Warrior ICV; the Warrior was a major step forward for the infantry, but its torsion bar suspension could not keep up with Challenger moving at full speed. *(Courtesy Richard Stickland)*

The turret and fighting compartment – general description

The turret is made up of steel plates, welded together to form a shell. Chobham armour panels are inserted in the front and sides, and then concealed behind a layer of thin steel cosmetic armour – and which is why these areas often sound hollow if tapped. Externally the turret roof is dominated by the commander's cupola and machine gun (MG). The loader's hatch is to the left of the cupola, with the rain cover for the loader's periscope forward of this. In front of the cupola is the gunner's sight window and MRS light source. Either side of the front is a five-barrelled smoke grenade discharger. On the right-hand side are two armoured barbettes; the front one contains the thermal imaging sensor head (TISH), the rear one the cooling pack. Two antenna bases are mounted towards the rear corners. In the top of the turret rear right is the bolted access hatch for the gun control equipment, and on

the left is the hinged access hatch for the turret batteries. Two stowage baskets with nylon covers are mounted on the rear sides, and a large stowage bin known as the 'coffin bin' is mounted on the NBC pack access door on the very rear.

The 120mm main armament (MA) barrel protrudes through a small opening in the front centre of the turret, and does not use a conventional mantlet; rather, the opening is as small as possible and the vulnerable areas are protected by internal flexible asbestos 'splash curtains'. Behind the barrel inside the turret are the breech and recoil mechanisms of the MA, these are connected to the gun mounting cradle, as is the coaxial machine gun (coax MG). The cradle is attached to the front turret walls on either side by a large pivot, these pivots are known as the gun trunnions and allow the MA to elevate or depress as required. Elevation is achieved by an elevation gearbox on the right-hand side, which reacts to either electrical or manual demands.

Around the turret walls are various electrical and mechanical boxes, controls and systems,

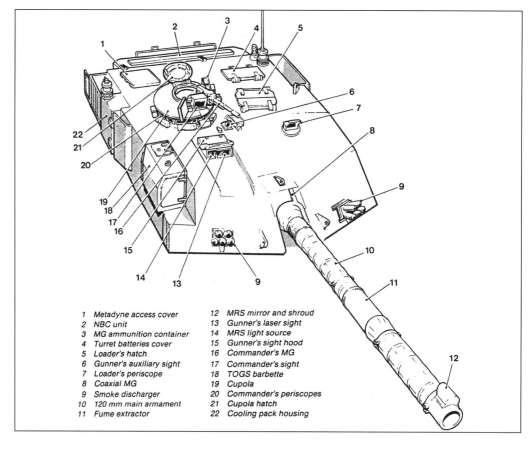

1	Metadyne access cover	12	MRS mirror and shroud
2	NBC unit	13	Gunner's laser sight
3	MG ammunition container	14	MRS light source
4	Turret batteries cover	15	Gunner's sight hood
5	Loader's hatch	16	Commander's MG
6	Gunner's auxiliary sight	17	Commander's sight
7	Loader's periscope	18	TOGS barbette
8	Coaxial MG	19	Cupola
9	Smoke discharger	20	Commander's periscopes
10	120 mm main armament	21	Cupola hatch
11	Fume extractor	22	Cooling pack housing

RIGHT The major turret fittings – external.

plus ammunition and other stowage; these are described in detail below. The gunner sits to the right of the gun cradle, with a number of viewing and sighting devices, plus the main firing controls; he is not provided with his own hatch. The gunner is primarily responsible for laying (aiming), firing – and if necessary correcting fire – with the MA and the coax. He enters before and exits after the tank commander, who sits immediately behind and above the gunner in the highest point of the turret. The commander's vision needs are provided by his all-round vision cupola which includes the hatch. He can override the gunner in certain functions, fire all weapon systems from his position (aka crew station), and monitor the loader. The loader is the third and last crew member to be found in the turret; he occupies the area to the left and rear of the breech, and is not only responsible for loading the MA and coax, but also for clearing MA misfires and coax stoppages, and is also the radio operator and makes the tea and sandwiches. He is the second in command of the tank in the commander's absence.

The turret must be able to rotate fully in either

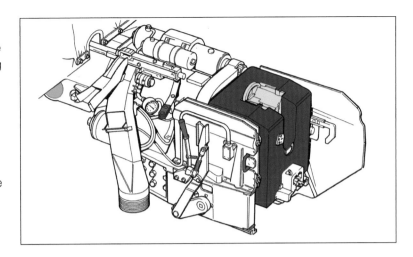

ABOVE The gun cradle, which allows the gun to elevate and depress by means of the trunnions (left hand shown in blue), and which also serves as the mounting platform for multiple components, including the recoil system and the coaxial MG. The breech ring is shown in green.

BELOW Looking from the loader's side of the turret, this is the right-hand turret wall with the gunner's seat and position on the lower left, and the commander's seat and position to the rear/right. This is a Mk 1 tank, as on a TOGS-equipped tank the APFSDS ammunition rack on the right would be replaced by the SPU. The red main and amber coax lamps on the gunner's Fire Control Box are shown.

direction around the hull: all-round traverse. In order to allow this, the hull has a large perfectly circular hole in the top, known as the *turret ring*. Immediately inside the turret ring is a toothed ring called the *turret rack*; this is in mesh with a pinion in the traverse gearbox on the right side of the cradle adjacent to the gunner. It reacts to either electrical or manual demands to traverse the turret either left or right, and at various speeds from extremely slow to very fast. Clearly, if the weight of the turret was sitting directly on the top of the hull it would be impossible to traverse, however good the gearbox was; therefore, between the hull and turret is a third ring known as the *turret* (or Roballo) *race*, made up of load-bearing ball bearings which support the weight and overcome friction, allowing traverse to take place.

Suspended below the turret is the traversing platform or turntable, usually referred to by the crew as the turret floor. This is suspended from the turret, and part of the suspension system is made up of curved and shaped tubular bars in the loader's side, which also act as a safety guard for the loader when the turret is traversing. The floorplate sits just above the hull

floor on a number of roller pairs; in each pair one is vertically aligned to take the weight of the turntable (but definitely NOT of the turret), and one is horizontally aligned to keep the turntable centralised. The floor itself and the space between it and the hull floor add protection for the turret crew in the case of a mine blast underneath the vehicle. In the very centre of the floorplate is the moving part of the RBJ, which remains in contact with the static part on the hull floor and is the means by which electrical signals, radio communications, and filtered air from the NBC pack is passed between hull and turret. The inside of the turret and the central part of the inner hull make up the fighting compartment.

The gunner enters the turret through the cupola hatch, climbing down past the commander's seat on to his seat. In front and to the right of the gunner's position is the traverse gearbox with the brick red traverse handle at the bottom. This has two positions, pull down for coarse or fast traverse, and push up for slow or fine. Traversing the turret by hand requires a lot of physical effort, so this method is generally only used for small or infrequent traversing, or when the electrically powered

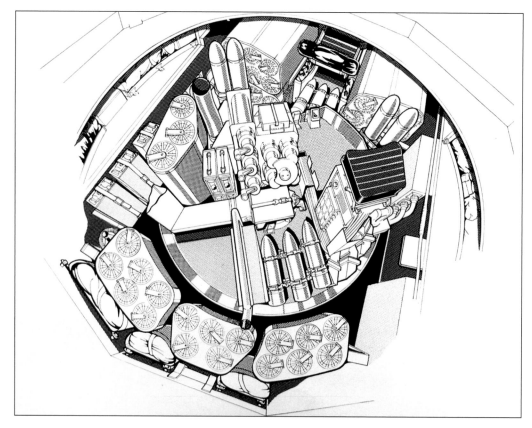

RIGHT The turntable or turret floor of a Mk 1 or 2 with the turret removed; much of the space is taken up by ammunition stowage, with projectiles in their racks and 7.62mm boxes on the left-hand sponson wall. All of the charge bins are also visible.

gear is not in operation. To the front and slightly left of the gunner's position is the black elevation handwheel; this is a handle mounted on a rotating disc, and is used to manually elevate and depress the mounting (and thus the guns). On the handle is a red firing switch, which is one of the many ways of firing the armament, but not the primary means – see the explanation of firing circuits below.

The gunner's feet rest inside a small floor plate, part of the turntable. All around the plate is a 3in or so raised lip to prevent the gunner's feet straying into the 'swept area' of the traverse – this would be very dangerous when using power traverse at speed, and was known as 'being eaten by the turret monster'; it wasn't funny when it happened. (When I was a sergeant in 3RTR in 1988, my loader managed to feed my driver to the monster on an exercise, which broke his leg, trapping him in the process. It took about 30 long minutes for me to extricate him, which could only be done by dismantling part of the turret.) In 1996 Cpl Steve Stobart of 2RTR broke his leg so badly in a similar accident in Canada that it came very close to being amputated; luckily it didn't come to that in the end but it shows that the system must be treated with respect. On the left of the floorplate is a footpedal, linked to a Bowden cable and which is the secondary (mechanical) firing system for the coax MG; to the right is a black foot firing pedal for the laser rangefinder, a throwback to Chieftain which is hardly ever used.

The loader has his own two-piece hatch, the same design as used on Chieftain. The hatch doors automatically lock in the open position and lie almost flat, and are released for closing down by operating plungers on the underside of the roof – and mind your fingers when closing the hatches as they are spring-loaded and quite heavy. The hatches can be padlocked from outside using a hasp. Once inside the turret the loader has more room to move around than any other crewman, and he tends to stand rather than sit, as his job requires him to move around quite a lot; during road moves under civilian regulations he should be head out and facing to the rear to assist with the control of traffic.

We will now delve in more detail into the various systems in the turret which we have

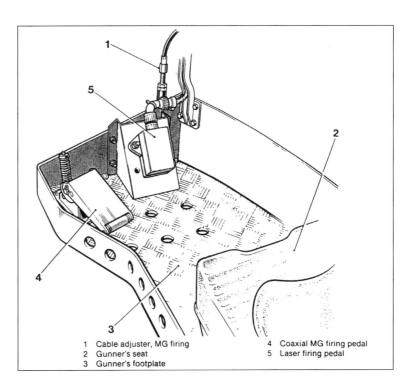

1 Cable adjuster, MG firing	4 Coaxial MG firing pedal
2 Gunner's seat	5 Laser firing pedal
3 Gunner's footplate	

ABOVE The gunner's footplate, with a raised lip all around it to prevent the gunner's feet from accidentally straying into the traverse. The coax MG foot firing pedal provides a secondary means of firing that weapon system, but the laser foot firing pedal next to it is very rarely used and is often disconnected to prevent accidental firing of the laser.

LEFT The loader's two-piece hatch in the open position. The locking handles can be painted a variety of colours, generally red, orange or yellow.

LEFT The loader's hatch closed and locked; the two handles on the rearmost hatch allow easy access from outside to conduct casualty evacuation.

ABOVE Projectile stowage racks in the loader's side, with 11 APFSDS in the vertical racks and 14 HESH/Smoke in the horizontal bustle racks. The box just visible on the left is the turret ration box, large enough to take the brew kit but not much else. The top of it has a non-slip tread plate to use when entering/exiting the turret. Note also the five boxes of MG ammunition strapped in on the hull side wall. The red 'gun ready' light is also visible, positioned facing the commander so he can see it illuminated as part of his immediate pre-firing check.

LEFT Empty stowage racks on the real thing – a Mk 2 with GRP charge bins. The quick-release straps hold the individual Fin projectiles in place, with a sliding bar over the top which holds all five in place. A well-drilled loader would use these projectiles to 'top up' the more convenient vertical racks during lulls in firing.

LEFT Practice ammunition unboxed and ready to go at Lulworth; SH/P shells are in the foreground, with DS/T behind. Practice ammunition was able to be used on much smaller ranges than the service ammunition.

touched on so far. A good place to start is with the machine guns. We can then look at the main armament, the gun control equipment, computerised and manual fire control, thermal imaging and the electrical systems and ancillaries. Some turret items are dealt with in Chapter 4, Survivability.

The coaxial machine gun and ammunition

Two machine guns are fitted to the turret of the tank. The models differ slightly but they are both 7.62mm-calibre guns from the General Purpose Machine Gun (GPMG) family. The gun used coaxially with the main armament is the L8A2 model. The mount for the coaxial machine gun forms part of the gun cradle in the 11 o'clock position when viewed from the rear. The very front of the barrel, the flash hider tube, protrudes through the hole at the front of the turret. When mounted, the loader can cock the gun using the remote cocking handle which

LEFT A Royal Hussars crew re-bombing their tank with DS/T bag charges on ranges in Germany.

L7A2

L8A2

L37A2

LEFT The L8A2 is used as the coaxial MG, and the L37A2 as the commander's MG; the latter can be converted, by the use of the L1A2 barrel (with adjustable gas plug, carrying handle and foresight), the butt, and the bipod, into the infantry or 'ground mounted' role. It then resembles the infantry L7A2, the main difference being the addition of the feed pawl depressor on the top cover.

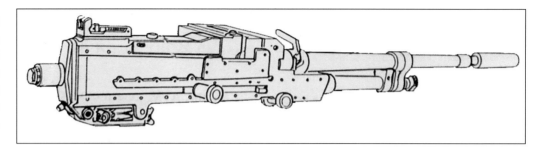

RIGHT The L8A2 version of the 7.62 mm General Purpose Machine Gun used as the coaxial or secondary weapon on Challenger.

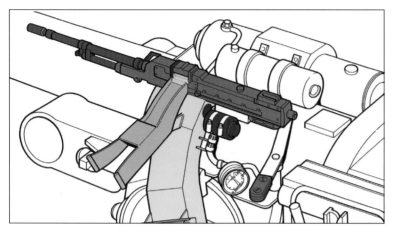

ABOVE The gun mounting for the coaxial machine gun on the top of the gun cradle. The feed tray is shown in light grey and is mounted to the spent cartridge case and link exit chute shown in yellow. The electrical firing solenoid is in green with the manual trigger extension in purple, and the remote cocking handle is in red.

BELOW The loader's view of the machine-gun mount – the ammunition feed tray has not been correctly adjusted as it should bear up against the silver feed tray on the side of the gun. Missing from the left side of this instructional stand is the rubber concertina hose – known by the crews as the donkey dick – responsible for depositing the spent cartridge cases and links into the collection bag under the gun.

forms part of the gun mounting. Ammunition belts are fed into the gun from the left-hand side, from the so-called banana bin on the left-hand turret wall, and is passed into the gun mechanism via an adjustable and removable feed tray, designed to continue to feed ammunition without snags even when firing on the move is taking place. In normal circumstances, the gun is fired electrically by the gunner using an electrical solenoid mounted to the left of the gun. A Bowden cable can be operated by the gunner using a hinged foot firing pedal should electrical power fail. A small trigger extension lever is also fitted allowing the loader to fire off the gun's action manually if required. When the gun fires, the spent cartridge cases are ejected through a slot in the underside of the gun receiver and fall away to a collection bag mounted underneath the gun cradle. The empty links from the belt are pushed out of the right side of the gun by the next round being fed; they are collected via a link exit chute where they can also fall away and join the cartridge cases in the collection bag under the gun. The empty links tend to become jammed up in this area and cause stoppages.

BELOW The ammunition used is known as 'One Bit', because of its designation as 1B1T – one ball, one trace. The disintegrating links are shown.

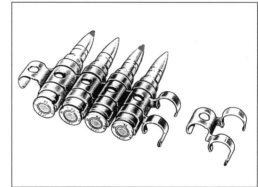

Turret electrical circuits

Most systems within the turret are electrical, and as a result there are literally miles of cables and connections running around the turret. As already mentioned, electrical and other signals are passed between the hull and turret using the rotary base junction or RBJ in the centre of the turret floor. A pair of 100AH batteries is mounted in the rear turret bustle on the left-hand side. These batteries are charged by the vehicle generators and are often called the radio batteries as they provide the necessary power for the radios to be used even when the ME and GUE are not running – the so-called 'silent watch'. Two master switches are used in conjunction with these batteries: one is the turret battery master switch which isolates all power from the batteries and is left on except when servicing the batteries, and the other is the radio master switch which allows current from the turret batteries to pass to the radios and radio harness system.

Gun Control Equipment (GCE)

The FVGCE No 11 Mk 3 electrical Gun Control Equipment (GCE) used on Challenger is a direct descendant of that introduced for service on Centurion. The most basic way of moving the gun and/or turret is by hand controls: the elevating handwheel and the traverse handle. During the Second World War it became common for tanks to be provided with a powered traverse system, and the Americans introduced a stabiliser system to allow shooting on the move. The British developed this concept on Centurion by providing electrical GCE. Many nations prefer to use hydraulic systems but the British Army made a conscious decision to avoid the fire and other injury risks associated with hydraulic pipes in the turret by opting for a purely electrical system. The equipment is sometimes referred to as the GCE, but the more commonly heard term is 'gun kit'.

The turret crew on Challenger therefore have a number of options for moving the gun and turret: by use of hand controls only – normally limited to small movements when the GCE is not operating, or during silent watch operations

at night. With the full GCE switched on, the crew have the ability to move the gun and turret by powered means and, if the tank is moving, to fully stabilise the gun in order to allow target tracking and shooting on the move. Control of this movement is exercised by either the gunner or the commander; both are provided with a component known as the grip switch and thumb controller. Physically they are both the same; however, the commander can always override the gunner simply by gripping on the grip switch. When either crewman grips his switch the system effectively becomes live and allows the thumb controller to be used; the crewman uses his thumb and moves the thumb controller in the direction that he chooses, with an increased demand being used for increased speed of response. This is particularly useful when laying the gun accurately in order to start an engagement, and indeed when tracking moving targets or shooting on the move.

ABOVE The turret batteries in the rear left turret bustle access is via a hinged door on the turret roof, so they are much easier to service than the hull batteries.

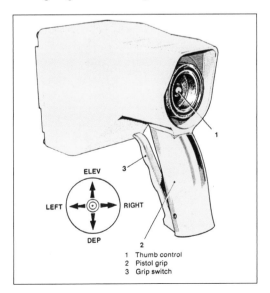

ELEV

LEFT — RIGHT

DEP

3

1

2

1 Thumb control
2 Pistol grip
3 Grip switch

LEFT The grip switch and thumb controller. The gunner and commander each have one of these components; however, the commander is able to override the gunner simply by gripping his grip switch. With the grip switch pressed the GCE becomes live and the crewman uses his thumb to cause the gun to traverse and/or elevate. The greater the demand placed on the thumb controller the faster the response.

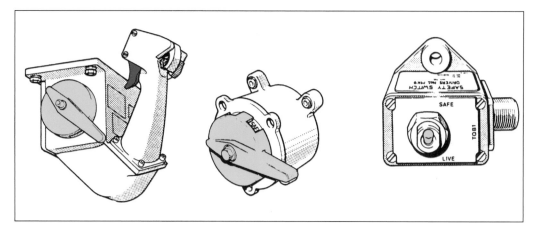

RIGHT The safety switches highlighted in yellow: from the left, the commander's, the loader's and the driver's. The commander's firing switch on his firing handle is shown in the correct colour red.

Safety switches are provided for three of the crew members; the driver has a two-position switch mounted on the underside of the glacis immediately forward of his hatch, which he must always set to SAFE when entering or leaving the cab; setting it to LIVE allows the GCE to be used. Similarly, the loader has a safety switch on the left side of his position on the underside of the turret roof, and this must always be set to SAFE prior to doing any work on or around the gun – for example working on the coaxial machine gun. The commander's safety switch when set to the OFF position has an additional safety feature in that it will switch off the Gun Control Equipment power supply unit and the metadynes. The gunner does not have a safety switch per se, but all the controls for switching on and off and fine-tuning the Gun Control Equipment are located in his station and these controls can also be used as safety switches.

RIGHT The major turret electrical boxes are shown in this diagram. Behind the commander's position in the right side of the turret bustle are the components controlling the power for the electrical Gun Control Equipment including the metadyne units (5, 6), which power the elevation and traverse gearboxes, and the power supply unit (8). The right-hand turret wall is almost completely taken up with various electrical boxes including the control panel for the electrical Gun Control Equipment. Shown as 12 on this diagram is the Turret Distribution Box (TDB), which contains the all-important connection for the boiling vessel. The Rotary Base Junction is 14 and the loader's safety switch is 11.

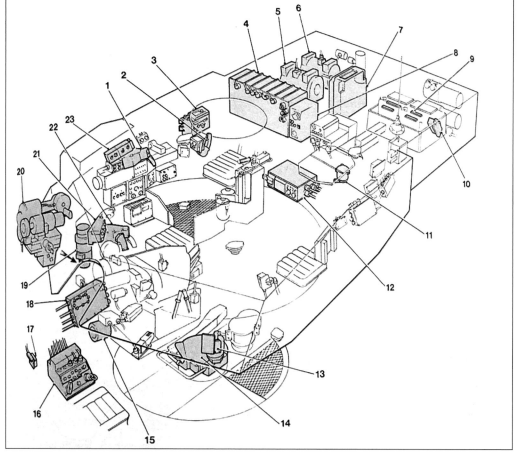

The vision cupola

The commander's cupola used on Challenger is the Cupola AV No 32 Mk 1. It is capable of all-round manual traverse and is fitted with nine x1 magnification No 40 periscopes. It is also fitted with a periscopic day sight for the commander, and a 7.62mm MG. The latter is used for anti-aircraft fire and to engage targets when the coax is unable to traverse on to them or is already engaging another target. Both the gunner and the commander use the cupola hatch for entry and egress into their turret positions. The hatch has four positions: fully opened; fully closed; an upright position; and a nearly closed or 'umbrella' position.

The commander's sight is the No 37 Mk 5 or Mk 6. This is mounted into the cupola from inside the turret and is protected externally by an armoured hood with a closable hinged armoured door. The sight has two magnification systems: a x1 window which overlaps with the

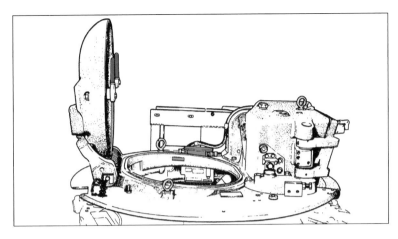

ABOVE The rotating part of the cupola ring: the commander's hatch is shown in the upright position, with the two spring-loaded clamping handles in red – these engage into two slots in the inner part of the ring, the left hand of these shown in orange. The green junction box provides connections for the electrical cables for the MG solenoid and the spotlight. The three rings shown in yellow are only needed when carrying out a cupola lift, and are not normally fitted.

BELOW 79KF36 at the RAC Open Day with the commander's hatch in the umbrella position. *(Courtesy Andy Brend)*

RIGHT The vision cupola with the nylon covers for the spotlight and MG ammunition stowage. Spent cases have been linked together to represent the ammo belt.

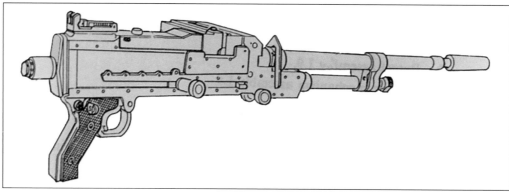

RIGHT The L37A2 MG is designed to be able to be rapidly converted into the ground role by the addition of the butt and bipod. For this reason the L1A2 infantry-type barrel with foresight is usually fitted, even in the cupola mount.

RIGHT The No 39 commander's sight shown dismounted and with the sight linkage transit bar fitted to the left side. Immediately behind this, the lever on the left changes the view between the x1 window and the x10 eyepieces. The graticule pattern is injected into the sight by the PRI through the rectangular window on the front right.

fields of view of the periscopes either side, and gives the commander 360° vision all round. Below the x1 window are a pair of movable, focusable heated x10 eyepieces used to observe fire and if necessary to engage targets through. The graticule pattern seen through the eyepieces is not generated within the No 37 sight, but is injected into the sight by means of a Projector Reticle Image or PRI, which is linked to the gunner's sight and hence to the gun cradle. Because the PRI is fixed to the underside of the turret roof this graticule pattern will only be viewable by the commander when the cupola is in the line-up position. At one stage it was the intention to fit Challenger either with a combined day/night sight (as intended for Shir 2), or to carry a separate image intensified night sight, which could be swapped as required. However, the introduction of TOGS rendered this unnecessary.

Nine Periscopes, No 40 Mk 2, are mounted

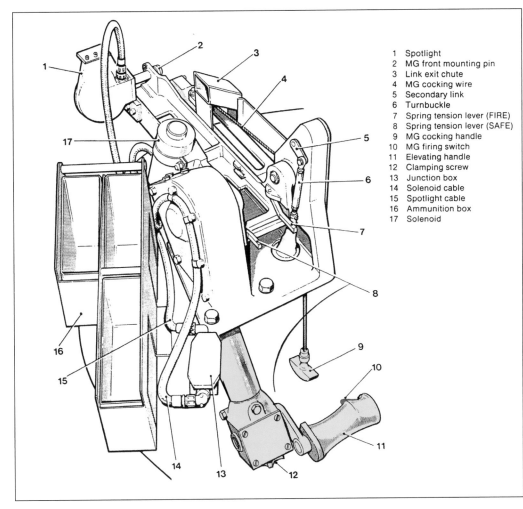

1	Spotlight
2	MG front mounting pin
3	Link exit chute
4	MG cocking wire
5	Secondary link
6	Turnbuckle
7	Spring tension lever (FIRE)
8	Spring tension lever (SAFE)
9	MG cocking handle
10	MG firing switch
11	Elevating handle
12	Clamping screw
13	Junction box
14	Solenoid cable
15	Spotlight cable
16	Ammunition box
17	Solenoid

LEFT The commander's MG mount, with the internal components highlighted in yellow. The rubber cocking handle and wire pulley can be seen at 9. Ammunition would be linked up to the gun from the three boxes, giving 600 rounds.

BELOW The small spotlight mounted to the front of the MG mounting; this could easily be switched on accidentally, which would give away the tank's position at night, and so was usually kept covered by a green nylon cover.

into the cupola from the outside, and are locked into position from within using yellow-painted locking devices. Each periscope includes a shutter device to prevent light from the turret escaping outside when operating tactically at night. Should the periscopes become damaged, up to two of them can be replaced from inside by pushing the damaged periscope outwards from the cupola and replacing them with an emergency No 41 periscope designed to be fitted from the underside of the cupola and locked using the red locking devices. Each of the periscopes has an individual washer and wiper system, and it must be said that the wiper system particularly has a reputation for being largely ineffective.

The commander's machine gun mounted on the cupola is the L37A2 model 7.62mm machine gun. Some 600 rounds of ammunition can be linked together in three boxes in the ammunition tray mounted to the left of the gun,

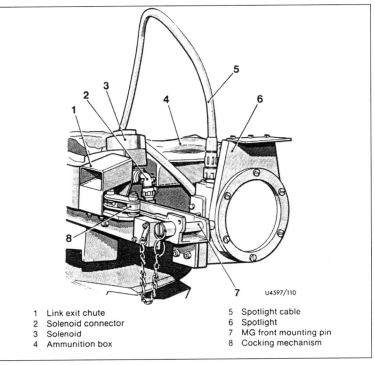

U4597/110

1	Link exit chute	5	Spotlight cable
2	Solenoid connector	6	Spotlight
3	Solenoid	7	MG front mounting pin
4	Ammunition box	8	Cocking mechanism

RIGHT The Commanding Officer of the QRIH, Lt Col Arthur Denaro, in the cupola of his tank 11B, at the moment the Gulf War cease-fire was announced at 08:00 on 28 February 1991 – he is wearing an NBC suit and holds his hunting horn! His map is on the inside of the hatch where the handles can be rotated to keep it in place, a very typical practice.
(Courtesy QRH)

BELOW The TISH: the very shiny black front lens was made of a special crystal material called Germanium, which allowed signals at the right frequencies to pass through on to the detector.

BELOW RIGHT Inside the TISH barbette, with the TISH lens looking skywards, showing off the Servo Trunnion Unit that it is mounted within.

on the outside of the cupola rotating ring. The gun is electrically fired using a solenoid on the mounting, and laid by the commander using the cupola traverse handle and the machine-gun elevating handwheel, which incorporates the firing switch. At the forward end of the MG mounting is a 100W 3½in white light spotlight; as it is quite easy to inadvertently switch the spotlight on from within the cupola – which could be very embarrassing or even dangerous for the tank commander at night – the sensible commander will keep the spotlight covered with the elasticated nylon cover provided until it is actually required.

Thermal Observation and Gunnery Sight (TOGS)

Being able to operate and fight at night gives a modern army a distinct advantage; Chieftain was provided with a 1950s technology infra-red or white light searchlight, but this had serious tactical and technical disadvantages and was never considered for Challenger. Rather, the future of night viewing was in an emerging technology called thermal imaging (TI), which detected the heat differential between vehicles, men and the surroundings. GSR (OE) 3845 of 19 June 1980 required the delivery

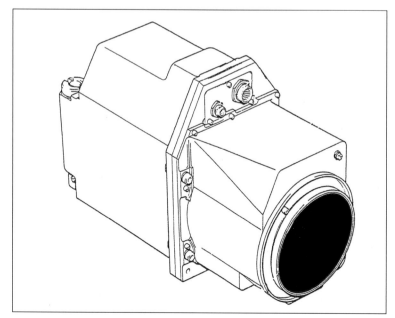

of a TI system for both the not-yet-officially ordered Challenger and Chieftain, in order to give the tanks 'a passive night and poor visibility system compatible with IFCS'. Barr and Stroud were awarded the contract in April 1981, and eventually 895 tank systems (for both tanks) plus spares were bought. The system was called the Thermal Observation and Gunnery Sight, or TOGS.

Before describing the TOGS system in detail we might first consider how thermal imaging in basic terms works. The thermal picture as seen through a thermal imager does not require light and so can operate in total darkness and conditions of poor visibility. Indeed, it should be thought of as a day/night system, and not merely used at night. It is a passive system and is very difficult for the enemy to detect, unlike white light or classic active infra-red systems. The 'eye' of the TOGS system is the Thermal Imaging Sensor Head or TISH, which is in effect a form of camera. Temperature control of the TISH is critical and this is provided by the Coolant Supply Unit or CSU. A thermal image sight can be likened to the human eye: the eye consists of a lens which collects light and passes it to the retina. This converts the light signal into an electrical signal, passing it to the receiving area of the brain via the optical nerve. The brain amplifies the signal and passes it to the visual area where it is

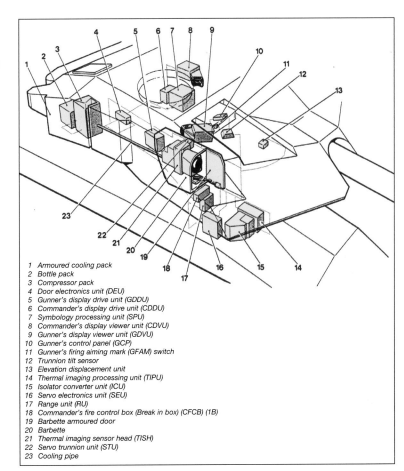

1 Armoured cooling pack
2 Bottle pack
3 Compressor pack
4 Door electronics unit (DEU)
5 Gunner's display drive unit (GDDU)
6 Commander's display drive unit (CDDU)
7 Symbology processing unit (SPU)
8 Commander's display viewer unit (CDVU)
9 Gunner's display viewer unit (GDVU)
10 Gunner's control panel (GCP)
11 Gunner's firing aiming mark (GFAM) switch
12 Trunnion tilt sensor
13 Elevation displacement unit
14 Thermal imaging processing unit (TIPU)
15 Isolator converter unit (ICU)
16 Servo electronics unit (SEU)
17 Range unit (RU)
18 Commander's fire control box (Break in box) (CFCB) (1B)
19 Barbette armoured door
20 Barbette
21 Thermal imaging sensor head (TISH)
22 Servo trunnion unit (STU)
23 Cooling pipe

ABOVE The TOGS components, known as LRUs or Line Replaceable Units. Fault finding could often only be carried out by swapping suspect LRUs with known ones from serviceable tanks, a major irritation for the crews concerned, as removing an LRU often meant that the whole system had to be recalibrated when it was replaced, a task of many hours.

LEFT The SPU adjacent to the commander's station with the lid closed to protect the switches and displays from damage. The CDVU and GCVU are also highlighted. The GDVU was fixed but the CDVU had to be moved out of the way in order to traverse the cupola.

converted into a picture that we can interpret. To function correctly the retina must be held at a constant temperature, and this is controlled by the blood flow.

To manufacture a thermal image sight, components of the eye need to be replaced with similar devices – lens, detector, amplifier, and visual display unit. Temperature control is achieved using High-Pressure Pure Air (HPPA). The part of the thermal image sight which requires precise temperature control is the detector. It is most efficient at around –200°C, at which temperature air turns into a liquid. The detector is therefore kept immersed in liquid air to maintain the correct and constant temperature. This liquid air is produced by a Joule-Thomson mini cooler which operates on the principle that air under high pressure,

if allowed to expand, will rapidly cool. High-pressure air is thus pumped through the mini cooler, which allows it to exit via a very small restrictor – only about one-fifth the thickness of a human hair; because this outlet is so tiny it is necessary to remove all possible contaminants that are likely to cause a blockage. Thus it can be seen that the air supplied must be both high-pressure and pure.

In order to move the TISH up and down when the gun moves up and down, the TISH is mounted in a Servo Trunnion Unit or STU. Signals are passed between the TISH and the SPU via the Thermal Imaging Processing Unit (TIPU) and the Servo Electronics Unit (SEU) which controls the STU. The SPU is the brains of the TOGS system and also serves to interface TOGS with CSS in order to allow full CSS engagements to take place using the TISH as the means of viewing targets rather than optically using the visual sights.

In order to view the thermal picture, the gunner and commander are both provided with 41mm Cathode Ray Tube Display and Viewer Units, the GDVU and the CDVU. These units are in effect miniature green light 625 line television monitors, and allow TOGS to be used both as a surveillance device and also in the gunnery mode; the field of view in low magnification is 265 x 177 mils. Although the crew are able to change the thermal picture between black-hot and white-hot and also to focus in on targets or areas of interest, the DVUs cannot be independently controlled so it is usual for the gunner to make the adjustments to suit him as he is the one firing the gun. (With TOGS the commander can fire the weapons with the same accuracy as the gunner, which is NOT the case when using visual systems.) Most of the controls used during an engagement – and indeed the calibration of the system – are mounted on the SPU, but those controls which the gunner must have access to in order to complete an engagement are duplicated on the gunner's control panel mounted adjacent to his firing handle. Should the Computerised Sighting System fail but TOGS still be available, the SPU can act as a reversionary ballistic fire control computer which will generate a Laser Aiming Mark and a Ballistic Aiming Mark to replace the MBS mark and ellipse respectively, thereby allowing engagements to take place.

BELOW A schematic showing the basic interfaces between CSS and TOGS; both systems could operate as gunnery fire control systems independent of the other, but integrating them was a complicated affair involving different computer languages and numerous complex calibration routines for the crew and REME. The TIPU contains a coaxial socket, allowing remote viewing or recording equipment to be connected into the system.

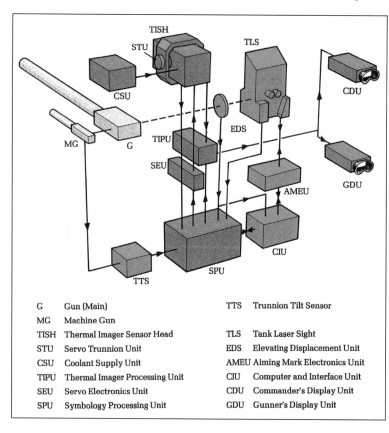

G	Gun (Main)	TTS	Trunnion Tilt Sensor
MG	Machine Gun		
TISH	Thermal Imager Sensor Head	TLS	Tank Laser Sight
STU	Servo Trunnion Unit	EDS	Elevating Displacement Unit
CSU	Coolant Supply Unit	AMEU	Aiming Mark Electronics Unit
TIPU	Thermal Imager Processing Unit	CIU	Computer and Interface Unit
SEU	Servo Electronics Unit	CDU	Commander's Display Unit
SPU	Symbology Processing Unit	GDU	Gunner's Display Unit

Engaging an enemy tank

According to the doctrine applied to Challenger, the main purpose of a tank is to destroy enemy armour; the secondary purpose is to provide close support of infantry. We will now go through the basic engagement sequence in order to fire at an enemy tank. Normally the ammunition of choice to do this will be APFSDS, but in this instance we will assume that the enemy tank in question is a basic T62 with no additional armour and therefore can be defeated quite easily using HESH. We are using only visual systems, so TOGS is not being used. Both gunner and the commander are scanning for targets, in this case using their visual sighting systems; the gunner will be scanning using x1 in his TLS and the commander using the x1 cupola periscopes and the window in his No 37 sight. Only when something of interest is observed will the crewmen look through their x10 eyepieces. This is because x1 gives them the widest field of view and the best chance to spot a target.

In this example we will assume that the commander spots the target first, and sets the engagement sequence in motion by gripping his grip switch and moving the gun and turret on to the target. As he does so he starts giving the fire order; in this case 'HESH, Tank … On.' Each word means something very specific. 'HESH' tells the gunner and the loader that it is a main armament engagement that is about to take place, and HESH is the ammunition to be fired; the loader will continue to load this nature of ammunition automatically without further orders from the commander until he is told to stop doing so. The word 'Tank' simply tells the gunner that the target he is looking for is a tank, and the commander will only say the word 'On' when the MBS mark is laid on or very close to the target to be engaged and he has released his grip switch, allowing the gunner to use the GCE to fine lay the gun.

As soon as he hears the first word of the fire order the gunner will lift the selector guard on his firing handle and push the selector switch over to the right in order to select the main armament. Selecting main armament charges the laser so that it is ready to be fired in a few seconds' time. When the gunner selects main armament APFSDS will be selected by default, so therefore the gunner needs to use his ring finger on his left hand and press the ammunition selector button twice until HESH is selected, and displayed in the left-hand eyepiece of the TLS; the commander is able to monitor that the selection is correct as it is also displayed on his Commander's Range Readout. As soon as the gunner has identified the target indicated by the commander he replies 'On', telling the commander that he is ready to continue with the rest of the engagement. Once the loader has completed the loading sequence and closed the breech, has picked up the next HESH projectile, pulled the loader's firing guard to the rear, and checked that the safety switch is set to live he will report 'Loaded'. When the commander is happy that the engagement can be continued he will issue the executive word of command: 'FIRE!'

While this is happening the gunner will be taking a very fine lay, laying the dot of the MBS mark on to the centre of the observed mass of the target; if the target is not fully exposed it is important that he doesn't try to guess where the rest of the target is, as it may be protected by an earth bank or similar; therefore he fires only at what he can see. As soon as the MBS mark is correctly laid on to the centre of the observed mass the gunner will press the laser switch, reporting 'Lasing' as he does so. As this is a static target being engaged within 1.3 seconds he will push the bottom part of the same switch down in order to demand autolay. These two actions will allow the computer and Interface Unit to carry out the ballistic calculation and generate the necessary information to lay the gun on the target.

When the gunner presses the lase switch an oval ellipse (oval) mark will be generated within the sight, and should fit neatly around the target. The size of the ellipse is based on the expected size of a T72 tank at the range that the laser has calculated, and therefore the gunner can do a very rapid check to see that the ellipse is of the correct size and is positioned correctly and snugly around the target. (If it is not so he will abort and re-lase

RIGHT The gunner has pressed the lase switch and CSS has injected an elliptical aiming mark into the TLS – the size of the ellipse depends on the range to the target and should fit neatly around a fully exposed T72 series tank.

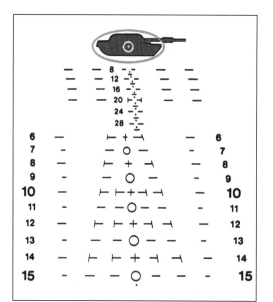

RIGHT The gunner has demanded autolay and the ellipse has displaced to the correct position on the graticule pattern at 800m, with aim-off included as calculated by the CIU. The gun and turret have not yet moved.

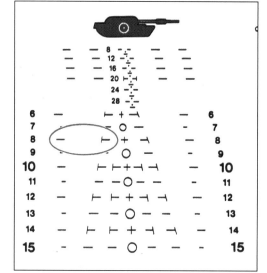

RIGHT With the gunner holding the autolay switch pressed, the GCE has 'driven up' to position the gun and turret in the correct firing position, and once more the ellipse is snugly positioned around the target. The gunner must pause for half a second or so as the gun settles into position before he can fire.

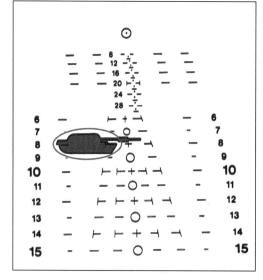

the target.) However, assuming all is well, when the gunner demands autolay the ellipse will displace within the sight to the correct tangent elevation and aim-off. In other words, it will move from its position around the target down on to the correct place on the graticule pattern calculated by the CIU. By keeping the autolay switch pressed the Gun Control Equipment will now take over and move the gun and the turret into the correct position for firing; the gunner will recognise this has happened when the ellipse is once more positioned snugly around the target – the gun is now laid ready to fire.

The gunner must wait for a fraction of a second to allow the gun to settle; as soon as it is settled the gunner can fire the first round, reporting 'Firing Now' as he does so, and squeezing his electrical firing switch on the 'Ow of Now' and so causing the round to be fired. If the target is hit and destroyed, the gunner will report 'Target' and the engagement can be terminated by the commander reporting 'Target Stop – check MRS.' As this is a HESH shoot, if the target is not hit the gunner and the commander will work together and conduct a series of corrections – line and/or elevation – in order to bring rounds accurately on to the target until it is destroyed. When firing KE ammunition the sequence is basically the same, but no corrections are possible because the round moves so very fast that observation of the fall of shot is just about impossible. If the first round misses in a KE engagement then up to two more rounds are fired; if after three rounds it has not been hit then the assumption is made that a system error has happened and the engagement is terminated.

OPPOSITE TOP 'Firing Now!' A Challenger fires during a firepower demonstration on Salisbury Plain. *(Courtesy Andy Brend)*

OPPOSITE BOTTOM 'Target Stop!' An Iraqi T55 burns during Operation Granby in 1991. Despite the criticism levelled at Challenger 1's gunnery performance in the annual NATO gunnery competition, in the Gulf War it performed admirably, and at ranges well beyond those specified.

Chapter Four

Survivability in combat

Challenger crews will be familiar with the 'survivability onion', a conceptual illustration that shows how to keep a tank and its crew safe. From a practical viewpoint, however, what was most important to a crew was the protection afforded by the Chobham armour, giving them the best possible chance of surviving a hit.

OPPOSITE 3 Tp C Sqn QDG in the Bosnian mud with the red Welsh dragon on the TOGS door. All the QDG Challengers remained in plain NATO Green for service with IFOR; some tanks had the lids of the coffin bins painted orange for air recognition. *(Courtesy Richard Stickland)*

The survivability onion

In old money the three main characteristics of a tank were always described as Firepower, Protection and Mobility. Only the latter remains, Firepower now being referred to as Lethality, and Protection has been replaced by a much wider concept called Survivability. In essence, achieving survivability can be likened to the layers of an onion: rather than just relying on simple physical protection in the shape of armour, the concept of survivability uses a layered method to prevent having to rely on armour protection at all. In order to survive in combat, the first and simplest way to avoid being killed is simply not to be there. This is normally achieved at the political level, for example bringing economic or political pressure to bear on an enemy rather than having to deploy a force. More recently it can involve long-range unmanned strikes, for example by using cruise missiles or unmanned aerial vehicles.

However, assuming that a force has to be deployed, the so-called 'boots on the ground', the next method to be employed is to prevent the enemy seeing you. This can involve measures such as strategic deception and reducing the electronic signature. At the tactical level it involves the correct use of ground and terrain to avoid being detected by the enemy, and also camouflage measures such as the colour that the tank is painted and the use of camouflage nets when halted. Another way of preventing the enemy 'seeing' you is through use of good radio procedures such as minimising radio transmissions and the use of codes to prevent the enemy discovering exactly where you are and what you intend to do.

If the enemy do detect you, however, they will attempt to attack and therefore the next level of survivability involves reducing the likelihood of being engaged by the enemy. The use of smoke and the agility of individual tanks will contribute to avoiding being engaged successfully. If these measures too prove fruitless and the enemy are able to engage, then the next layer of the onion is to avoid being hit: in other words, the enemy is able to open fire but simply cannot manage to hit you. Again, good use of terrain and tank agility, including the rapid transition from being static to moving, will make it difficult for the enemy to strike. If these measures fail and the enemy *do* strike, it is now that you have to rely on your armour protection to keep out their penetrators. But as was made clear in the introduction, the correct use of the Whittaker Arc to determine where best to place armour protection on a vehicle also means that not all parts of the vehicle can be armoured equally. So there will always be areas of the vehicle that are more vulnerable than the others, usually the underside, the rear and the top. And of course the enemy may develop weapons which are able to overmatch your armour protection, in which case you will be penetrated, but yet you must avoid being killed.

To do this, you can use active and passive measures to limit the effects of that penetration. Most modern tanks, Challenger being no exception, use a spall liner to limit or reduce the behind armour effects that take place after penetration. Other passive measures include the use of fire detection and suppression systems, and specific protection can be given to fuel and ammunition to prevent fires and explosions. Finally, in the category of avoiding being killed, we can also consider such actions as crew first aid and the effectiveness of the casualty evacuation chain.

BELOW The survivability onion is simply a conceptual way of thinking about how to keep the crew and vehicle safe.

DO NOT BE: THERE

- SEEN
- ENGAGED
- HIT
- PENETRATED
- KILLED

Do not be seen: paint and camouflage

Paint and camouflage is applied to the tank in order to make it more difficult for the enemy to see us. In the modern era, such paint will almost invariably be in a matt finish, with a colour or colours chosen to match the average background that one expects to fight in. When Challenger left the production line it was painted in NATO Green paint, which had infra-red reflecting (IRR) properties to make it more difficult to detect using night vision aids. The application of a camouflage pattern using NATO Black IRR paint was left to units, with the pattern being dependent entirely on the person or persons painting the tank, using the basic rule that one-third was to be black and two-thirds green. When 7th Armoured Brigade,

ABOVE LEFT The front registration plate measures 550 x 100mm; the rear plate measures 200 x 350mm. Officially, each white stripe of the convoy plate is meant to be 50 x 200mm, with the black stripes slightly narrower at 35 x 200mm, but these were generally painted in the same width or replaced by a white square bearing the squadron symbol and vehicle callsign in black.

ABOVE RIGHT (TOP) National flag symbol.

ABOVE RIGHT (BOTTOM) Sub-unit and call sign.

followed by 4th Armoured Brigade left for Saudi Arabia in 1990 and early 1991, every effort was made to paint them in the standard British desert camouflage colour known as Light Stone before they left Germany.

Do not be seen/engaged/hit: fire positions and agility

A great deal of attention is spent during training in making sure that individual tank commanders and tank formations (troop, squadron and larger) move effectively over the ground in order to increase their survivability by not being seen, or engaged, or hit, by an enemy. The basic rule to be obeyed is that of fire and movement: an individual tank should never move unless it is covered by the fire of at least one other. When leaving one fire position to move to another, the tank will, if in actual contact or under enemy observation, carry out a manoeuvre known as jockeying; that means that the tank will always reverse out of a fire position, move off a significant distance to one side or the other, and then and only then move forward. This is to prevent the enemy shooting you if you simply drive forward over a skyline from where you were.

When moving into a static fire position, the

RIGHT Fire positions. On the left are three positions seen from the side, and on the right, the enemy's view. The top position is fully exposed. Finding some natural cover puts the tank in a hull-down position, reducing the exposure to about 33%. Better still, a slope which still allows the crew to fire in depression will reduce exposure still further, to about 25%. Good fire positions therefore make it much harder for the enemy to spot or engage you.

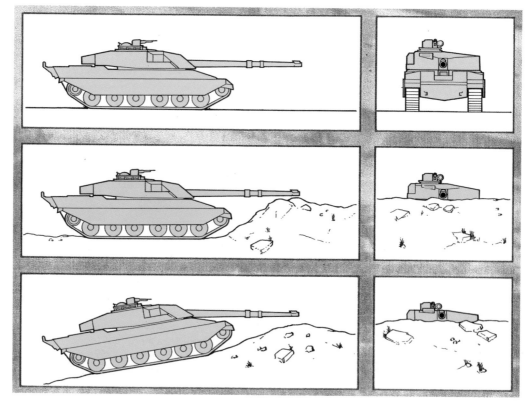

commander, gunner and driver must all work closely together as a team in order to move into the best position in respect of the likely whereabouts of the enemy. Ground will be chosen that provides cover from fire as well as cover from view, and wherever possible the tank will position itself on a reverse slope position. This will mean that only the gun, the gunner's sight and the cupola are visible to the enemy over the top of the crest, whilst allowing the crew to fire at the enemy effectively. The less of the tank that can be exposed to the enemy the better; when observing the ground ahead the commander will often adopt what is known as a turret-down position, where none of the vehicle can be seen by the enemy, with only the commander's sight (or better still just the commander's head with his binoculars) visible to an observant enemy.

Do not be hit: smoke

Either side of the front face of the turret are a pair of multi-barrelled smoke grenade dischargers, MBSGD No 18 Mk 1. Each has five barrels set at a fixed elevation of 25° and, when used together, electrically discharges ten smoke grenades up and away from the

tank to provide an immediate smokescreen for local protection. Before firing the turret should be traversed to ensure that the grenades explode between the tank and the enemy, and the lateral spread of both sets when fired together is 1,800 mils, or about 100°. Three types of smoke grenades may be used: the L5 (white smoke) and L7 (green) are similar, using HexaChloroEthane (HCE) as the smoke-producing compound. Both of these have an

ABOVE One of the two banks of MBSGD; the pair of barrels was mounted uppermost.

BELOW Bindon range at Lulworth; a CR1 demonstrates the firing of L5 or L7 smoke grenades from the MBSGD.

eau-de-nil painted metal body, with a nominal calibre of 66mm, and begin to emit smoke once they have landed on the ground where they burn for about 90 seconds. The L8 White Phosphorous grenade gives a more instant but shorter duration screen, bursting when still in the air but only emitting smoke for about 60 seconds. Each barrel is covered by a rubber cup, keeping the grenades (or the empty barrels) dry until required; the cups are ejected with the grenade. The firing buttons, one for each bank, are located forward right of the commander's position on the turret side wall.

Do not be penetrated: Chobham armour

The introduction into service of Chobham armour was the single most important leap forward in armour protection technology since the introduction of the tank in 1916. As this type of armour is still in use on service vehicles in the British Army, only a partial story can be told here, to avoid giving away precious military secrets. However, with the agreement of the Defence Armour Security Committee, a little more of this story can now be told.

The perennial problem facing armour designers is to produce an armour that is capable of withstanding an enemy attack as well as being as light and as low bulk as possible – not to mention inexpensive and easy to produce. This problem is made more difficult to solve when the enemy deploys a number of different anti-armour threats. As we have seen, these threats can be broadly divided into KE projectiles, which use a combination of dense material and very high speed to defeat the target, and CE weapons, which use some form of explosive attack. Potentially the most devastating of these is the High Explosive Anti-Tank (HEAT) type of warhead, employed as hand-held infantry weapons such as the RPG, or in a larger form fitted to tank projectiles and guided missiles. Wargames conducted during the 1960s indicated that the HEAT threat was increasing, and that around 70% of tank casualties could be expected to come from such attack. Therefore, the modern armour designer must seek to develop and deploy armour which is capable of withstanding both forms of attack equally well.

In the early 1960s RARDE was wrestling with this problem. One of their scientists, Dr Gilbert Harvey, was the leading light behind the invention – or more accurately serendipitous discovery – of a revolutionary new way of putting armour together that could do just this. It is not absolutely clear whether Harvey came upon the idea of using a number of different materials in layers purely by accident, but composite armours were being used to protect naval vessels in the nineteenth century, so it may be that this historical knowledge gave him the idea to layer dissimilar materials together in a type of sandwich. Another factor which almost certainly influenced him was the knowledge that air gaps within armour systems can often be beneficial. Whatever the exact construction, the idea of such a composite armour is to cause the threat to malfunction, to break up, to burn out, to be deflected, or in short to lose energy before it could reach the interior of a tank where the crew and the vital components are located.

Unfortunately, armour material that was good at defeating or breaking up an incoming KE projectile was often of no use when trying to defeat a HEAT attack, which could penetrate hundreds of millimetres of conventional armour. Some materials show promise but cannot be made to work as armour; for example, polypropylene plastic could actually give more protection from HEAT than the equivalent weight of steel but in order to do so was far too bulky and vulnerable in other ways to be useful. Harvey made a particular breakthrough when he was investigating systems that could store fuel safely so that the fuel would not ignite if hit by a projectile. He noticed that the honeycomb structure of the fuel storage system tended to deflect the HEAT 'jet' and also to absorb some of its energy.[1] He realised that if the different layers of material could be arranged at different angles, then the high-energy HEAT jet which was trying to take the shortest possible path through the armour could be deflected and possibly dissipated. It appears that this breakthrough was made some time before 1963, as that was when Harvey made a secret

---

1   Often but erroneously referred to as 'burning' through the armour.

patent application, although many years were to elapse before the armour could be optimised and developed to the point where it could be fitted on to a service vehicle. Amazingly, this armour recipe was also at least as good as conventional steel armour at resisting KE attack – the philosopher's stone had been discovered. Most of the 1960s were spent in trialling different recipes, and although the exact dates are still classified, it is known for instance that Trial 47 took place on 20 April 1966 and Trial 70 was conducted in May 1967. By 1969 it was mature enough to be taken forward into design options on a modified Chieftain or on to a new tank – but exactly why it was as good as it was remained a mystery, and more research effort was then directed at explaining the protection mechanism. This was critical, as without understanding why it did what it did, the scientists would be unable to predict theoretically how it might be developed, and would be restricted to trial and error.

Because RARDE was at one time located at Chobham Road, Chertsey Common, the armour which was sometimes referred to in the early days as 'Harvey's armour' was most commonly called Chobham armour. This appears to have been unofficial, at least

initially. By the late 1960s it had been given a new codename for secrecy reasons – Burlington – and the protection mechanism was being referred to as the Burlington Principle. Burlington was described by the UK security policy in August 1969 as 'that armour designed to give exceptional protection against penetrating jets from shaped charges [HEAT], formerly known as Chobham armour'. Another and even more secure codename, Moustache, dealt with those people who not only knew

ABOVE The FV4211 side packs contained an early version of what was to become Chobham armour. Twelve boxes were mounted along the full length of the hull side; the curved bar at the front is to deflect trees etc. that might get stuck between the pack and the hull proper.

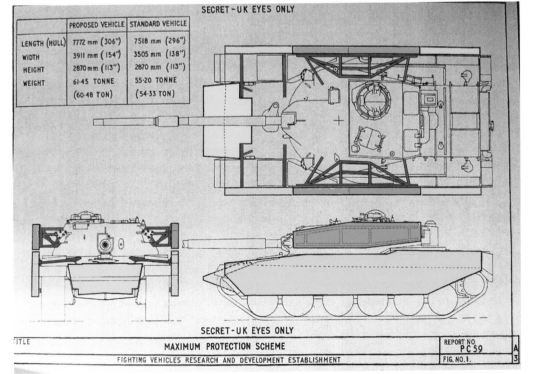

	PROPOSED VEHICLE	STANDARD VEHICLE
LENGTH (HULL)	7772 mm (306")	7518 mm (296")
WIDTH	3911 mm (154")	3505 mm (138")
HEIGHT	2870 mm (113")	2870 mm (113")
WEIGHT	61·45 TONNE (60·48 TON)	55·20 TONNE (54·33 TON)

TITLE	MAXIMUM PROTECTION SCHEME	REPORT NO. PC 59	A 3
	FIGHTING VEHICLES RESEARCH AND DEVELOPMENT ESTABLISHMENT	FIG. NO. 1.	

LEFT Chieftain Mk 5/2 with Burlington appliqué panels – this is the maximum protection scheme.

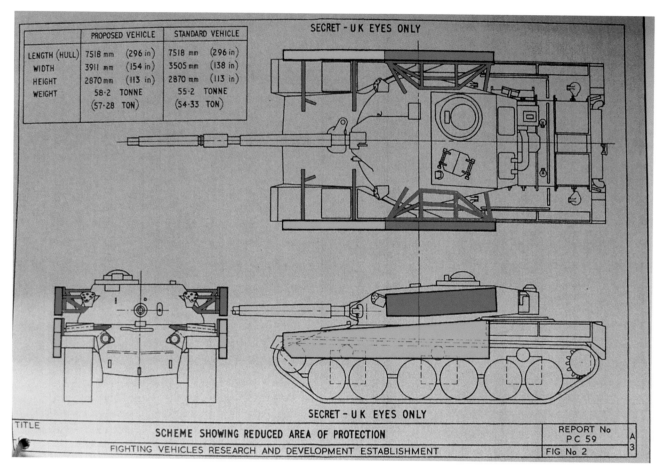

	PROPOSED VEHICLE		STANDARD VEHICLE	
LENGTH (HULL)	7518 mm	(296 in)	7518 mm	(296 in)
WIDTH	3911 mm	(154 in)	3505 mm	(138 in)
HEIGHT	2870 mm	(113 in)	2870 mm	(113 in)
WEIGHT	58·2 TONNE		55·2 TONNE	
	(57·28 TON)		(54·33 TON)	

TITLE	REPORT No	A
SCHEME SHOWING REDUCED AREA OF PROTECTION	PC 59	
FIGHTING VEHICLES RESEARCH AND DEVELOPMENT ESTABLISHMENT	FIG No 2	3

ABOVE Chieftain Mk 5/2 with Burlington appliqué panels – this is the reduced protection scheme which omitted the nose cone and provided lesser HEAT protection for the crew.

what the armour could do, but understood how it worked and also the research attempts being made to defeat it – 'counter-Burlington'. The name Chobham then resurfaced to become the name by which it will always be known, and which was used when its existence was first announced publicly; this was because the codename Burlington (but not the technical details) was assessed to have been compromised, so the name Chobham came back into official use.

On 17 June 1976 the British Defence Minister Roy Mason announced that 1,225 Shir 2 tanks were to be produced for the Shah of Iran and these tanks were to be equipped with a new type of armour. He stated that this new armour would 'represent the most significant achievement in tank design and protection since the Second World War … weight for weight it gives significantly better protection than all existing armours against attack by all forms of anti-tank weapons'. This was as far as the government were prepared to go in announcing details of the new armour,

and although worldwide speculation at the time and since was rife, officialdom quickly closed ranks and no more was said, although in some ways the genie was out of the bottle.

Back to 1969: the armour had been developed to the point where it could be fitted on to a vehicle, and the British military establishment was wrestling with the decision as to when to deploy it and thus reveal its existence. There were two options: fit it as an appliqué system to a modified Chieftain; to those in the know this was Chieftain Mk 5/2, and for the rest this designation was protected by the codename Almagest. The other option was to develop an entirely new vehicle, designed from scratch to mount the armour as part of the vehicle structure, and it was this approach that led to FV4211 being developed. But the fastest way of meeting the Soviet threat was to design an appliqué system, and like all such systems, it was both difficult to integrate and added a lot of weight. The individual components of the appliqué were designed to be manhandled by the crew,

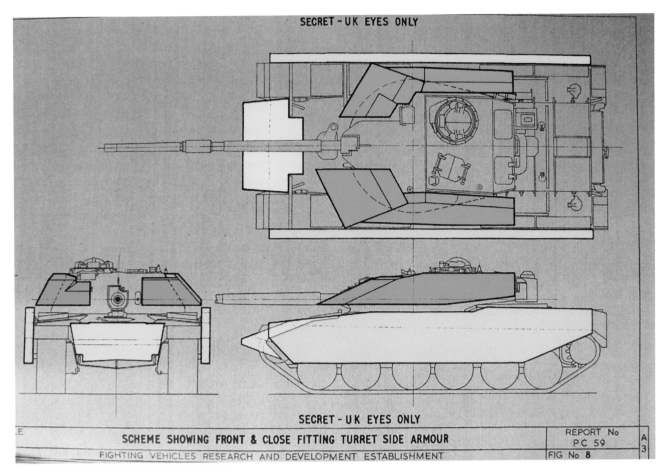

SECRET - UK EYES ONLY

SECRET - UK EYES ONLY

SCHEME SHOWING FRONT & CLOSE FITTING TURRET SIDE ARMOUR

REPORT No PC 59

FIG No 8

FIGHTING VEHICLES RESEARCH AND DEVELOPMENT ESTABLISHMENT

ABOVE The bespoke 'close fitting' scheme shows where the turret shape of Shir 2 – and thus Challenger 1 – derived from.

and were referred to as 'biscuits'. Two main appliqué schemes were suggested: a £12,000 6-tonne maximum protection scheme including full-length hull side plates, turret side plates and a glacis nose cone incorporating some bar armour; or a £7,000 3-tonne reduced scheme of much smaller hull and turret side plates only, able to protect the crew from hand-held RPG weapons but not from the larger-calibre guided weapons. Other schemes proposed a much more integrated close-fitting solution for the hull and/or turret armour. The generals in the British Army of the Rhine (BAOR) were consulted as to whether they would accept the tanks being prepared for Chobham but not actually mounting it in peacetime, reducing the weight to 57 tonnes. Not surprisingly, given the expectation of a future war to start with a surprise Soviet attack, they would not countenance such a time-consuming method, 'dressing the tanks for war' as it was referred to. In 1970 £1 million was allocated for developing Burlington for use on Chieftain 5/2, and a discussion ensued over whether

the British Army might consider purchasing a 'half generation' of between 250 and 400 Burlington-equipped tanks to partially replace the Chieftain fleet from 1975. As it was, Chieftain 5/2 was never fielded and Chobham would only make its debut on Challenger, albeit via FV4211.

Britain chose to share information on Chobham with its closest NATO partners, and the first such sharing took place in late 1964 or early 1965, when the USA were told of its existence by Sir Solly Zuckerman, who was the chief scientific adviser both to the MOD and the government. In 1966 possible collaborative research was being discussed but nothing came of it, partly because the US scientists were pursuing very different armour research, and partly because they were very sceptical about the claims being made – it seems that they thought that it all sounded too good to be true. In 1970 talks were resumed, and the British, by then close to mounting it on service tanks, were not convinced that they were getting anything useful in exchange. This

MEMORIES OF CHOBHAM ARMOUR

WO1 (ASM) Mark Cobham, Royal Electrical and Mechanical Engineers (REME)

All of those chosen to have involvement with Chobham armour underwent the Chobham Armour Repair Team (CART) training. This consisted of a background briefing by the resident experts in Chertsey who were responsible for the research and development of the armour in its early years – and I still feel privileged to have had the presentation from these guys – to understanding the true composition of the armour. This also included the Top Secret videos of it on test being fired at using all types of ordnance. In one case nearly 40 different types of ammunition from small to artillery shells were fired at a single turret. The results were hugely impressive.

Once we'd been CART'ed we were sworn to secrecy and given a secret codeword to use. This allowed one to know with confidence who we could discuss Chobham with. This became part of the cloak-and-dagger whispered exchange that took place everywhere I went on my marathon tour around the UK mentioned below. It got quite funny at times, with conversations usually beginning in true 'Allo 'Allo fashion with something like 'listen very carefully, I shall say zis only once' – before getting down to the serious business.

Later I was serving with an off-shoot organisation of the old REME Technical Services BAOR, but based in the UK at Chertsey and known as Maintenance Support Group UK or MSG(UK). By then REME Technical Services BAOR had become MSG (Germany). We were alerted by our sister unit in Germany that virtually the whole fleet of Challengers that had ever been based in Germany had undergone an upgrade/refurbishment of the TOGS thermal imaging and gunnery system in the early 1990s at base workshops. One of the tasks involved accessing the inner workings/mounting of the TISH barbette, and this in turn necessitated partial removal of the cosmetic armour panel immediately over the adjacent Chobham armour. An enterprising mechanic decided to save time and simplify his task by cutting through and then peeling back a small section of the cosmetic plate, thus exposing the necessary area without having to actually remove anything. This was in the days after the initial 'flap' about keeping Chobham secret, so the corporate memory of the need to do this had dimmed somewhat. The result was that, much later on, it was suddenly realised that there was potentially a large number of Challengers rolling around Germany, and by this time many had found their way to Canada or back to the UK, with partially exposed and even possibly compromised armour.

My job was to rapidly visit every location in the UK where such tanks were based, stored, operating, on ranges etc, in order to inspect each one as quickly as possible. Fortunately we discovered that there was no exposure of the armour but some of them were extremely close! My 'pull up a sandbag' story for the remainder of my career always included the fact that despite my specialist area being wheeled vehicles, I had worked on every single Challenger based in the UK, something none of the dyed-in-the-wool armour guys could ever claim!

did not stop full disclosure happening, one source noting that the *quid pro quo* was that Britain was given over-fly rights for Concorde. The British also approached the Federal Republic of Germany in March 1970 under the codename Buckhorse, with a view to seeing if the Germans were interested in mounting the armour on Leopard 2, but were told that the design was too far advanced to be altered. It appears that the British logic was to offer it to the Germans in order to ensure that it would be mounted on a future Anglo-German collaborative tank. As it was, the first combat tank to mount Chobham armour was Challenger.

When tanks are made of homogenous pieces of armour, whether cast or rolled, it is very difficult to change or enhance the protection of these vehicles other than by adding appliqué armours to the outside of the existing structure. However, with a modular system such as Chobham, it is possible to remove the entire functional part of the armour and replace it with an updated or threat-specific new version. Partly for this reason and partly for reasons of convenience in production, the Chobham armour packs used on Challenger are bolted into steel frames that make up the structure of the tank, and then covered by fairly thin metal plates known as cosmetic armour (or 'what you see is not what you get!'); for this reason parts of the tank often feel hollow when being walked on. This method of construction, however, brought its own problems in terms of retaining the security of the armour, as it would be a fairly simple task to break through the cosmetic armour in order to investigate the secrets beneath. So the Chobham armour deployed had to be very carefully looked after to maintain the secrecy; indeed, when the tanks were in transit they were accompanied by armed guards, and when in their hangars in the barracks in Germany, armed guards once again were deployed to protect them and to prevent any unauthorised intrusion. In order to reduce this security burden, a number of tanks were built as training Challengers, so designated as they did not have the Chobham armour fitted but instead had dummy armour packs to make up the correct weight of the vehicle.

Do not be penetrated: appliqué armour packs

There is a constant battle between the attack and the defence; that is, between ammunition trying to destroy a tank and armour trying to prevent that happening. When the tank is designed, the armour used takes into account the most likely enemy and its weapons that that tank is going to face; indeed the General Staff Requirement will always state these conditions. If the most likely enemy deploys a new type of weapon, or the tank deploys to face an enemy that was not expected, then the armour may need to be augmented in some way. This was the case when Challengers deployed to the Gulf in 1990.

Plans for the use of British armour involved the possibility of having to fight within the confines of Kuwait city. Fighting In Built-Up Areas (FIBUA) as this was known doctrinally at the time (or as the soldiers preferred to call it FISH – Fighting In Someone's House), is a dangerous operation for armour and requires very careful tank and infantry cooperation, as the tanks themselves are very vulnerable to short-range, inexpensive and low technology weapons such as the rocket propelled grenade (RPG). RPGs can penetrate through a lot of conventional armour and this threat was particularly worrying for the British planners.

Therefore the decision was taken to up-armour the British tank fleet prior to active combat operations, with the order placed for 216 sets on 23 October 1990. Armour packs were rapidly developed, manufactured and shipped out to the Gulf where they were fitted to the tanks shortly before ground operations commenced on 24 February 1991.

These packs consisted of two elements: first, VARMA side armour Chobham packs replaced the normal aluminium bazooka plates and extended two-thirds the length of the vehicle in order to protect the crew and the ammunition. Secondly, ROMOR-A Level 1 Explosive Reactive Armour (ERA) blocks were fitted to the toe plate of the Challengers, because of the likelihood of being hit there at short range by RPG. The toe plate ERA was designed by RARDE Chertsey, with the construction of the frames carried out at ROF Nottingham. Each mounting kit weighed ¾ tonne, and comprised a 1in mild steel frame (and which therefore added no meaningful protection without the ERA). The frame fitted at the bottom to the front tow hooks, and was bolted to the glacis at the top using a 75mm bolt in either side. Dozer tanks could not mount the toe armour. Each frame had four compartments, each compartment was designed to take six ERA blocks, four small

BELOW **Before: only the side plates have been fitted to this tank. It awaits the toe-plate armour.** *(Courtesy Nige Atkin)*

LEFT During: an empty frame fitted to the toe plate and ready to accept the blocks; note the ever handy S10 respirators, in case of gas attack. *(Courtesy Dennis Lunn)*

CENTRE During: a member of the 2RTR Armoured Replacement Squadron fitting the ERA blocks into the frame, which is painted in the red oxide preservative finish. *(Courtesy Nige Atkin)*

and two large. The small blocks measured 310 x 195 x 20mm, and the larger blocks 385 x 195 x 20mm. The two centre compartments came with the four lower blocks in place, but the others had to be fitted after the frame was mounted on the tank. Each block had a hole drilled through at each corner in order to bolt the blocks to the frame. The configuration was:

2 x small	2 x small	2 x small	2 x small
2 x large	2 x large (fixed)	2 x large (fixed)	2 x large
2 x small	2 x small (fixed)	2 x small (fixed)	2 x small

Each of the packs took about 48 hours of hard work to fit on to the tanks by the crews with REME assistance, and the nature of the work was made more unpleasant as at this stage of the air war the crews frequently had to adopt the state of NBC Black: that is wearing their NBC suits and respirators. There were not enough armour fitting instructions to go round and so some errors were made, including at least one crew that was known to have fitted the ERA boxes the wrong way round; what is not known is if this mistake was found and corrected before the ground war started.

Do not be killed: charge bins

Three types of charge bins may be fitted to Challenger. The first of these are Glass Reinforced Plastic (GRP) water jacket bins which are a direct descendant of, indeed almost identical to, those used on latter marks of Chieftain. A total of 42 individual charge cylinders are available to the crew; each cylinder can take either one KE or two CE charges. Surrounding the cylinders is a mixture of water and antifreeze pressurised to 7 pounds per

RIGHT A GRP charge bin, with cylinders to hold 5 KE or 10 CE bag charges. The lids are made of a semi-transparent plastic allowing the loader to see which type of charge is in which cylinder.

RIGHT The transparent 'Stage V' closure lids
used with GRP charge bins. On the side wall of
the hull is the vehicle fire warning horn, linked
in to the fire warning sensor loop around the
powerpack compartment. The engine/turret
breathing handle is just visible to the left, above
the open container.

square inch; should the internal water jacket be
punctured by hot fragments, the pressurised
water/coolant mix will first of all cool the
incoming fragment, and secondly douse the
affected bag charge with pressurised water and
putting out a possible fire.

Following vulnerability trials on Chieftain with
GRP bins, a new system of Armoured Charge
Bins (ACB) was introduced, being fitted from
tank number 265, 78KF80; early trials were
conducted using 4030/3 prototype V3B3 from
1984 on. Rather than deal with the effects
of a penetration of the charge bin (don't be
killed), the intention here is to prevent the bag
charges being struck by fragments in the first
instance (don't be penetrated). Therefore, all
the charge bins are made of armoured steel
between 10mm and 25mm thick, designed to
prevent fragmentation from piercing the bag
charges. By managing to increase the number
of charges held in the vertical rear hull bins
from 17 to 26, only one replenishment bin of 12
cylinders needed to be fitted into the front hull;

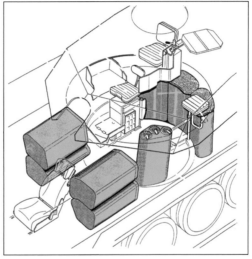

LEFT The layout of
GRP charge bins in a
Mk 1 or 2 Challenger.
Because of their size,
the cupola must be
removed in order to
change them. The four
horizontal bins behind
the driver's position
were in effect used as
a replenishment store
for the others, as they
could not be accessed
easily.

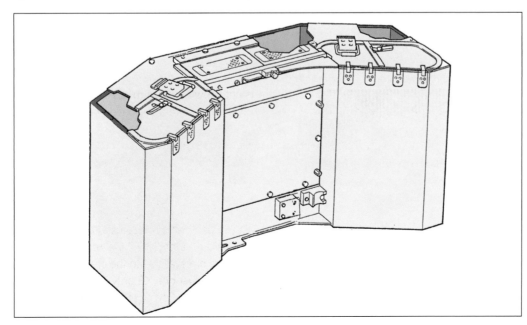

LEFT Some 26
charges can be held
in the hull rear bins;
the outside ones
have hinged doors
that open upwards,
whereas the centre
container has
sliding doors. Inside
are spring-loaded
cylinders to take the
individual charges.

LEFT Four KE charges are visible in the rear hull bin of a Mk 3; the thickness of the steel can be appreciated. To avoid potential dangerous mismatches, only one type of KE round was allowed to be stowed on a tank at a time. The white canvas handles allow the charges to be pulled out quickly and loaded.

BELOW Armoured charge bins; a variety of different closures were used, from rotating knobs to both hinged and sliding doors.

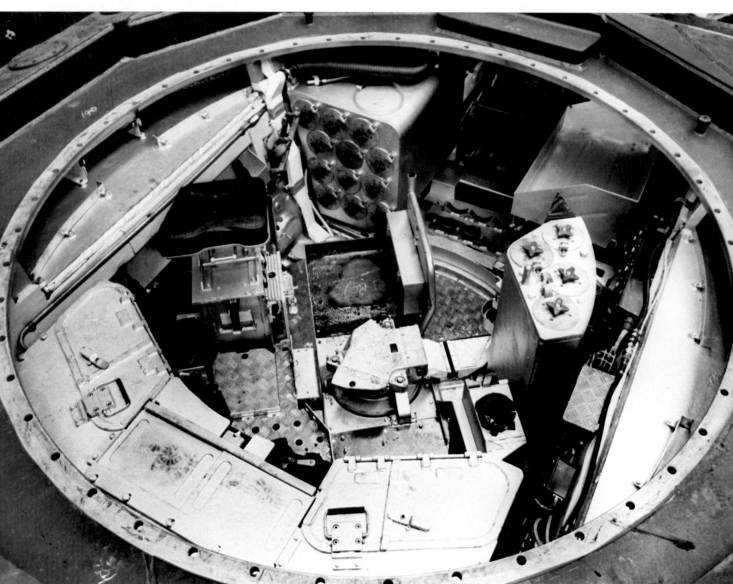

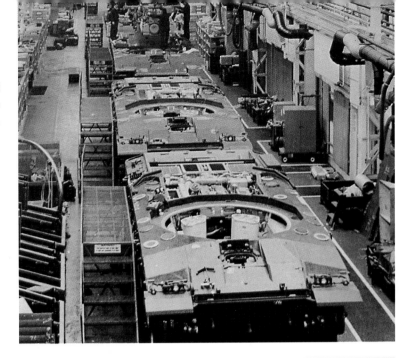

RIGHT Challenger hulls on the production line at Leeds, with two of the three rear hull GRP charge bins already installed.

in addition, the number of ready cylinders on the loader's floorplate bin was increased from 3 to 4. The first unit to receive vehicles fitted with ACB was the Blues and Royals (RHG/D), the fifth Challenger regiment.

When Challenger tanks deployed to the Gulf in 1990 a policy decision was made that wherever possible all tanks should be of the latest Mk 3 build standard. However, as over 50% of the total British Challenger fleet was to deploy to the Gulf, there were not enough Mk 3 tanks to achieve this. The decision was then made to retrofit armoured charge bins in place of the GRP charge bins to those Mk 2 vehicles which had deployed.

A major constraint was the size and weight of the GRP charge bins; normally the charge bins in the hull – that is all of them except the ready charge bin – are fitted into the hull of the tank during assembly on the production line. The GRP bins themselves weighed between 66 and 145kg. There was no question of being able to remove turrets in Saudi Arabia in order to do this, therefore the new system would have to allow the old charge bins to be removed and the new charge bins to be fitted with only the cupola removed. Because of this constraint it was not possible to simply fit the existing design of armoured charge bins from the Mk 3 vehicles. Instead a new modular design was developed and 90 kits were manufactured at Barnbow, in which rectangular boxes each containing two charge cylinders were produced and which could be connected together to form larger banks of charge bins which could be mounted in the required positions. Some 24 Mk 2 tanks were fitted with the bins before hostilities began. After Operation Granby was over, a number of other Mk 2 tanks were retrofitted with the same design of bins in order to use up the remaining stocks that had been manufactured.

RIGHT Changing the GRP charge bins for the Mk 2 (ACB) modification in Saudi Arabia meant removing the cupola, in order to create a hole large enough for the removal and fitting.

Chapter Five

Challenger crew

Four men inhabit the inside of a Challenger tank. Despite the best effort of the designers, not to mention all the impressive operating systems and clever technology, the efficiency and combat effectiveness of the tank ultimately relies upon the skill of its crew and how well they work together.

OPPOSITE Challenger crews of 14/20H in the Gulf in 1991. The hoops over the tanks are to allow the use of camouflage nets.

The crew

The four-man crew of the Challenger all have very specific roles and responsibilities; however, the key point for the crew to remember is that the tank will only be at maximum efficiency if they work as a team. This is something that can only be learnt by hours of practice on exercise and during other training activities. Each person in the crew will have their own strengths and weaknesses, and it is the function of the crew commander to understand this and to bring all four together in a way that will maximise the efficiency of the tank. The most important single part of the crew is the tank commander's brain; he should know exactly what he wants to do and he must train his crew to carry out his requirements as rapidly and accurately as possible, whilst avoiding possible causes of confusion. Sometimes these activities can be reduced to drills: a set sequence of activities that are practised in the same manner over and over again until they become second nature. Other tasks, though, will require more direct communications and each crew will develop its own preferred style of

talking to each other in order to communicate effectively – although guidance is given during gunnery training, for example, this is not necessarily rigidly followed and some crews are more formal than others.

Usually, the driver is the junior member of the crew. Often referred to as the 'cab rat', his is generally the most physical of the crew positions. As well as being responsible for the driving aspects, he is also the man responsible for most of the maintenance activities to be carried out on the systems contained within or mounted to the hull. This is referred to as Driving and Maintenance, or D&M, sometimes irreverently referred to as Dirty and Mucky. D&M is frequently heavy work; lifting the engine louvres, raising the radiators, and adjusting the tracks all require a degree of physical strength. There are numerous tasks that have to be completed according to a set servicing schedule. A number of tasks must be completed in order to confirm that the tank is safe and fit to be moved: this is referred to as the First Parade. During halts, however short, the driver must leave his cab and carry out checks, particularly on oil levels and on

RIGHT The driver's seat with him shown in the upright position for driving opened up. When closed down, the backrest is dropped rearwards and the shoulder rest and head rest adjusted upwards to allow him to use the periscope. In an emergency the backrest can be dropped flat to allow exit rearwards into the turret.

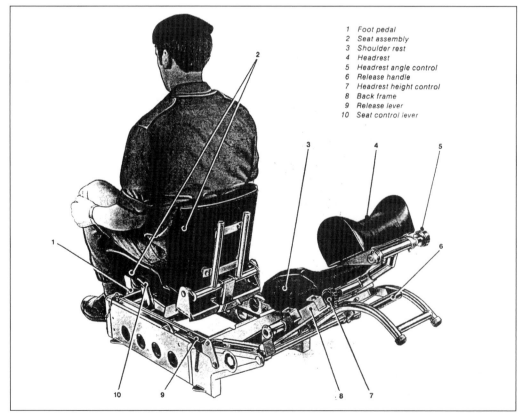

1   Foot pedal
2   Seat assembly
3   Shoulder rest
4   Headrest
5   Headrest angle control
6   Release handle
7   Headrest height control
8   Back frame
9   Release lever
10 Seat control lever

the suspension; for example, to ensure that the road wheel hubs are not overheating and that the wheel nuts are not becoming loose. Any faults he finds will be rectified immediately if possible and, if not, must be recorded in his notebook for later rectification. He will also report any serious faults to his tank commander. These so-called Halt Parades are carried out many times a day. At the end of the day the driver will conduct the Last Parade, again checking all around the tank for faults and serviceability. The maintenance/servicing schedules also lay down checks and servicing to be carried out on a weekly, monthly and sometimes quarterly or yearly basis, or when a certain mileage has been reached. This will include such activities as the routine cleaning of the air cleaner elements, changing of the oil and fuel filters, adjusting the tension of the tracks, servicing the batteries and the lubrication (greasing) of many of the moving parts.

The driver's seat is bolted to the floor in the centre, with the squab immediately underneath the access aperture. It is adjustable and has two basic positions, one to allow opened-up driving and the other for closed-down. In the latter case, the seat is dropped backwards until it is almost fully reclined, and the shoulder rest and head rest adjusted upwards to suit the driver's height and preference, and to position his eyes close to the periscope lens. To allow the driver to move into the fighting compartment, or for him to be evacuated in an emergency, the seat can be dropped down fully.

The gunner is the other junior member of the crew. His basic training to become a Crew Gunner will last approximately six weeks, and will teach him not only the techniques of firing all the weapons systems in the turret, but will also teach him how to maintain them, including the stripping, cleaning and reassembling of the main armament and the machine guns, as well as servicing the recoil system; the correct use of the Gun Control Equipment; sight adjustment; and general

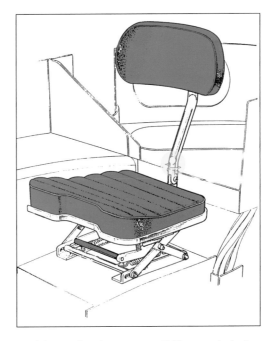

LEFT The gunner's seat: the (orange) lever on the lower front allows the preferred height setting to be chosen. The backrest is shown, and which fits into a socket (cream circle) in the commander's footplate behind the seat cushion. The backrest can be swivelled against the turret wall when not required.

servicing and maintenance activities conducted within and on the turret. Just like the driver, when he discovers faults he will either rectify them immediately or record them and report them.

The gunner's seat is situated forward of the commander's footrest, and the seat cushion can be raised or lowered to suit his height; there

RIGHT The loader's seat was a simple padded cushion on a frame that mounted on to his protective rail/knee guard; inside the knee guard was a narrow document case. The T-piece foot rest was almost never fitted.

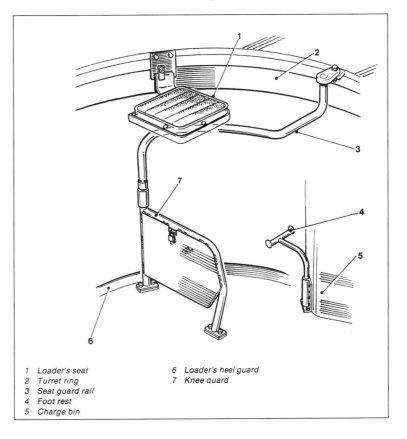

1	Loader's seat	6	Loader's heel guard
2	Turret ring	7	Knee guard
3	Seat guard rail		
4	Foot rest		
5	Charge bin		

drivers don't bother fitting the backrest, but sit back against their commander's legs.

Although known as the loader, the third member of the crew has the additional task of being the tank's radio operator. Although both the driver and the gunner will also have obtained basic qualifications as radio operators, it is the loader who is mainly responsible for making sure that the radio systems within the tank are correctly maintained and that the radios are operating properly. In addition to his radio operating tasks, the loader is also responsible for loading both the main armament and coaxial machine gun, the replenishment of ammunition, clearing any misfires and stoppages on the weapon systems, and, as the Boiling Vessel (BV) is located in his side of the turret, also makes the tea and sandwiches for the crew.

The loader tends to stand rather than sit, and he has a simple square seat pad which is a green vinyl-covered padded cushion on a metal frame. The seat can be clipped on to the horizontal section of the tubular safety rail and to the turret sill, so it can be easily removed and stowed out of the way when in action. If ammunition is not being carried, the seat pad can be rested on top of the projectile racks on the turret sill to allow him to travel with his head out. A T-shaped foot rest that fits into a socket at the rear of the ready charge bin is part of the tank equipment, but it's a nuisance so is generally left back in barracks.

The tank commander is the senior member of the crew and is responsible for everything that happens in his tank. The rank of a tank commander in a regiment will range from corporal to lieutenant colonel. Within a tank troop there are three tanks, commanded by a corporal, a sergeant, and the troop leader will usually be a lieutenant or sometimes a staff sergeant. (As I can testify, as a young corporal at the age of 23, being given command of a Main Battle Tank is a

ABOVE A very battered loader's seat on an Operation Granby tank in March 1991; it has been (sort of) repaired with that most useful commodity, very tough masking tape known as 'black nasty' or 'Harry Black'. The seat clips on to the safety rail – which the loader's boot is resting on – and also into the elongated slot in the turret sill. This is a Mk 3 tank as it has the Armoured Charge Bins fitted.

are six positions available in 1in increments, although of course the headroom diminishes with each raising. A simple backrest is provided, and is swivelled out of the way when entering and exiting by lifting it slightly and rotating it until it lies against the right-hand turret wall. Many

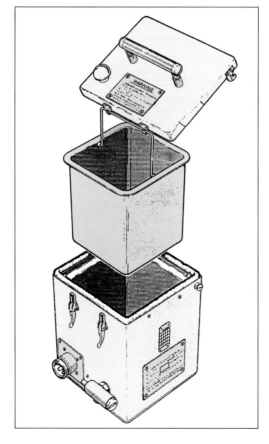

LEFT Usually described by the crew as the single most important piece of equipment, the Boiling Vessel is able to heat food and water. It cannot be mounted when in action though, as the Vent Tube Loader can hit it when the 120mm gun recoils. It is also important to ensure that it does not leak into the charge bins.

major event. For many it is the culmination of all
that they have worked towards for the previous
years.) As the tank commander will have spent
some considerable time as a driver, gunner
and also as a loader, he already has a wealth
of experience in the three tank trades. With
the purpose of formalising this experience and
knowledge, and to qualify as a tank commander
in order to earn the substantial extra pay that
goes with these new responsibilities, he must
attend the tank commander's course. This lasts
around 12 to 14 weeks and takes place at the
Royal Armoured Corps centre of excellence at
Bovington, with the gunnery phase (the best bit),
taking place at Lulworth.

Having qualified as a tank commander,
our young corporal becomes responsible for
everything to do with a Challenger tank weighing
nearly 70 tonnes and worth around £1½ million;
he is also responsible for the routine training and
supervision of the other three members of the
crew. He can be expected to take his tank on
a number of field exercises every year, probably
spending at least 6 and as many as 12 weeks in
the field. Every year, his squadron will deploy to
the NATO tank ranges at Hohne, where they will
spend two weeks conducting live firing training.
Every other year, his squadron will deploy to
BATUS, the British Army Training Unit Suffield,
in Alberta, Canada, where they will conduct
an intensive three-week period of live fire and
manoeuvre exercises which are as real as the
British Army can provide short of actual war.

The commander's seat is situated under
the cupola. The whole seat unit can be raised
and lowered using a pump handle on the left-
hand side; a small hydraulic reservoir is situated
immediately behind the handle, and this has
a control knob on the top used to lower the
seat; when the knob is turned, the weight of the
commander will cause the seat to quickly drop to
the lowest position. The worst feature about the
commander's position is the very small footplate;
he is unable to move his feet around very much,
and this is made worse if you have big feet like

BELOW **The hydraulically operated commander's seat was a decent design,
but the small size of the commander's footplate often led to knee pain, as
the commander was unable to move his legs very far. The circular inset
shows how the backrest could be raised up and locked into position to
provide extra height, a useful facility.**

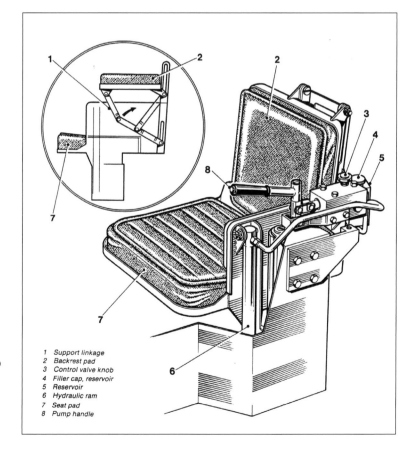

1 Support linkage
2 Backrest pad
3 Control valve knob
4 Filler cap, reservoir
5 Reservoir
6 Hydraulic ram
7 Seat pad
8 Pump handle

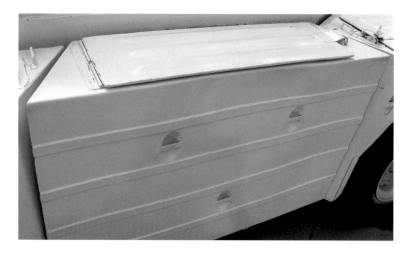

the author; over time this can cause the knees to lock and become painful. On Operation Granby, many commanders could scarcely walk after three days mostly spent in this position.

Stowage

When Challenger was introduced into service, one of the most frequent criticisms voiced was that there was insufficient stowage for all the various tools and items that the crew would have to carry. Chieftain was fairly well supplied in this area, as it had nine external stowage bins. Challenger, however, only had two, and despite the Challenger tool kit being somewhat smaller than that on Chieftain, stowage space was at a real premium. Officially, each item had its own dedicated stowage space on the tank as detailed in the stowage plans issued and which are reproduced below. However, these plans did not take into account all the various additional items that the crews needed to have with them, particularly such items as the

ABOVE The Ferret bin used on the turret right side; the side we can see here is the outside on the Ferret but is used as the inside on Challenger, being bolted on to studs welded to the side armour. The bin measured a maximum of 38in wide (29in inside), 24in deep, and was 8½in wide. It was generally used as the commander's personal bin, the other three crew using the coffin bin.

BELOW This Challenger at Ashchurch displays another common stowage modification, in the shape of a Chieftain rear hull bin bolted to the side of the coffin bin; note that the Chemical Decontamination/Oddy gun holder has been relocated next to it. *(Courtesy Michael Shackleton)*

amount of food they were expected to carry (often five days' worth), spare NBC equipment, the amount of water that was really needed on the tank (not only for washing and feeding but also for topping up coolant), and the quantities of washing kit and clean clothing required to allow the crew to operate on the tank for an extended period.

In time, the users found sensible expedient methods to add extra stowage containers to the tank. In particular, it was common practice to fit one of the 94in-long rear hull bins from Chieftain along the left side of the turret, and to fit another stowage bin (taken from a Ferret scout car but used 'inside-out') to the right-hand side of the turret below the commander's cupola. Other methods included fitting a large basket made of angled steel and wire mesh to the left turret side. Eventually this practical approach was officially endorsed, by the provision of additional and well-designed lightweight mesh bins to fit along the left-hand turret side wall and also on the right side of the turret between the two TOGS barbettes.

LEFT A KRH Challenger in Bosnia, showing the Ferret bin in use with one of the external fire extinguishers mounted on it. Note the 4th Armoured Brigade 'fat rat' on the TOGS barbette. *(Courtesy Richard Stickland)*

BELOW Mks 2 and 3, front left, three-quarter view.

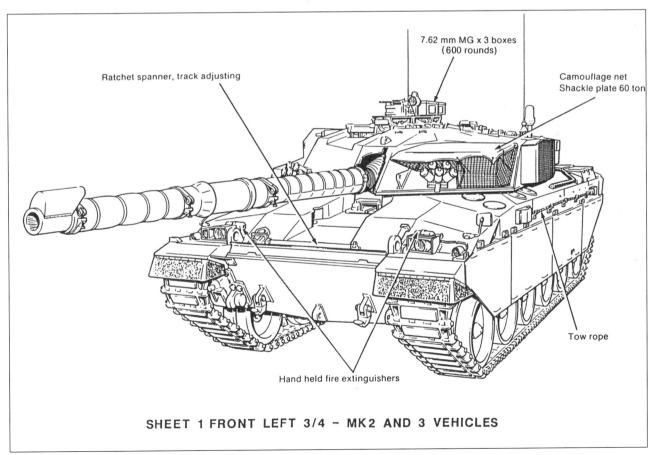

7.62 mm MG x 3 boxes (600 rounds)

Ratchet spanner, track adjusting

Camouflage net
Shackle plate 60 ton

Tow rope

Hand held fire extinguishers

SHEET 1 FRONT LEFT 3/4 – MK 2 AND 3 VEHICLES

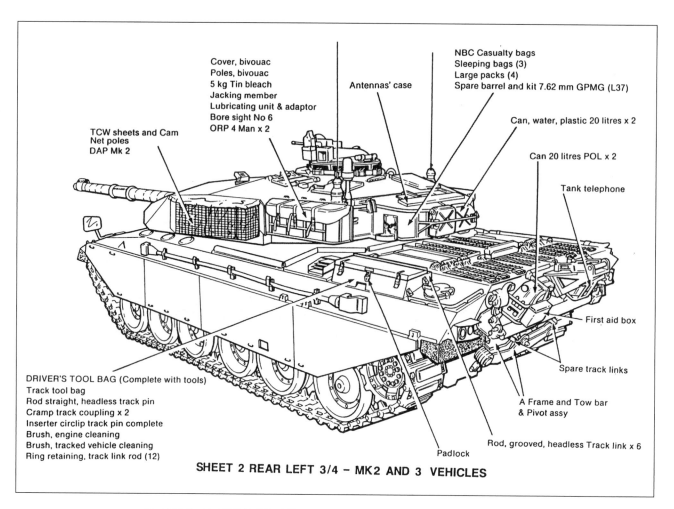

Cover, bivouac
Poles, bivouac
5 kg Tin bleach
Jacking member
Lubricating unit & adaptor
Bore sight No 6
ORP 4 Man x 2

Antennas' case

NBC Casualty bags
Sleeping bags (3)
Large packs (4)
Spare barrel and kit 7.62 mm GPMG (L37)

TCW sheets and Cam
Net poles
DAP Mk 2

Can, water, plastic 20 litres x 2

Can 20 litres POL x 2

Tank telephone

First aid box

Spare track links

A Frame and Tow bar
& Pivot assy

DRIVER'S TOOL BAG (Complete with tools)
Track tool bag
Rod straight, headless track pin
Cramp track coupling x 2
Inserter circlip track pin complete
Brush, engine cleaning
Brush, tracked vehicle cleaning
Ring retaining, track link rod (12)

Padlock

Rod, grooved, headless Track link x 6

SHEET 2 REAR LEFT 3/4 – MK2 AND 3 VEHICLES

**ABOVE Challenger
Mks 2 and 3, rear left,
three-quarter view.**

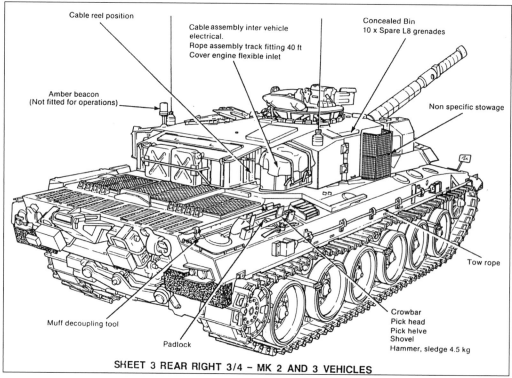

Cable reel position

Cable assembly inter vehicle
electrical.
Rope assembly track fitting 40 ft
Cover engine flexible inlet

Concealed Bin
10 x Spare L8 grenades

Amber beacon
(Not fitted for operations)

Non specific stowage

Muff decoupling tool

Padlock

Tow rope

Crowbar
Pick head
Pick helve
Shovel
Hammer, sledge 4.5 kg

**RIGHT Challenger
Mks 2 and 3, rear right,
three-quarter view.**

SHEET 3 REAR RIGHT 3/4 – MK 2 AND 3 VEHICLES

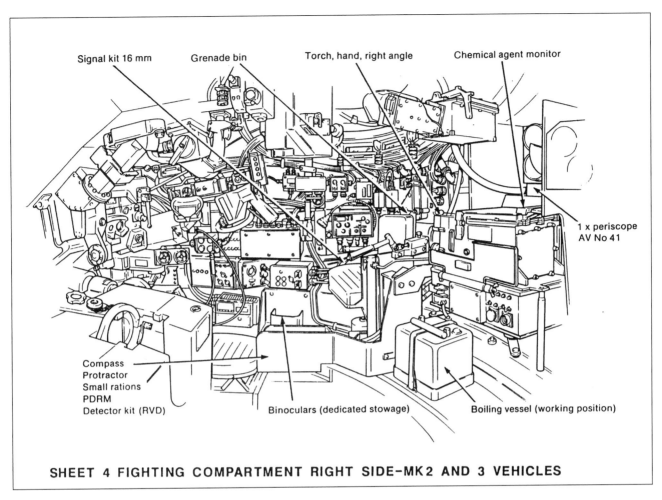

Signal kit 16 mm Grenade bin Torch, hand, right angle Chemical agent monitor

1 x periscope
AV No 41

Compass
Protractor
Small rations
PDRM
Detector kit (RVD)

Binoculars (dedicated stowage) Boiling vessel (working position)

SHEET 4 FIGHTING COMPARTMENT RIGHT SIDE—MK 2 AND 3 VEHICLES

SA 80

Magazine, electrical primer 0.625 in L10A1 Contact electric tester firing circuit
Oiler hand ½ pint flexible spout
Firing, needle assembly spare
Torch, right angle
First aid box

7.62mm MG 2400 rounds

Gun retaining plate stowed

Grenade bin

Rations
Brew kit
Mugs

Gunner's tool bag
Hoist assy breech block
Injector oil and petrol
Tool alignment vent tube loader
Tool cleaning breech block chamber
Spanner box No 7 ORD 0.775 in AF
Adaptor, firing circuit tester
Spare CPU)
Spare PBU) in signals satchel
Spare RPU)

Gauge contact protrusion No 6
Tool opening breech block
Cap, plug, protective dust and
moisture seal,
Tool obturator assembly
Electronic maintenance case

7.62 mm MG x 5 boxes
(1000 rounds)   Spare barrel 7.62 GPMG (L8)

SHEET 5 FIGHTING COMPARTMENT LEFT SIDE — MK 2 AND 3 VEHICLES

**ABOVE Challenger
Mks 2 and 3, fighting
compartment, right
side.**

**LEFT Challenger
Mks 2 and 3, fighting
compartment, left side.**

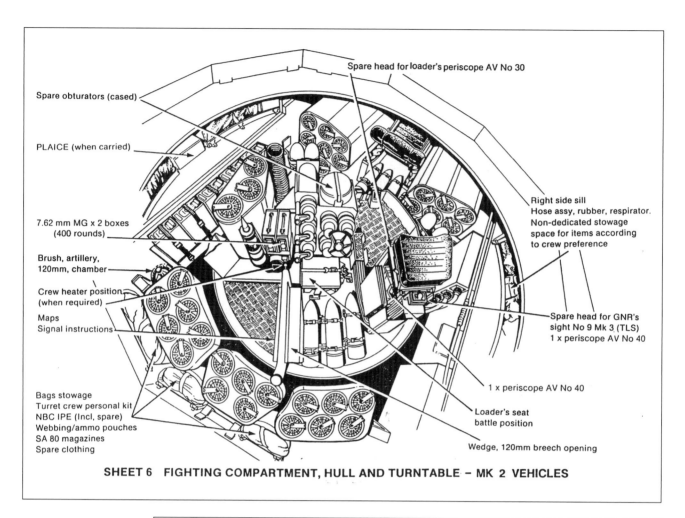

Spare head for loader's periscope AV No 30

Spare obturators (cased)

PLAICE (when carried)

7.62 mm MG x 2 boxes (400 rounds)

Brush, artillery, 120mm, chamber

Crew heater position (when required)

Maps
Signal instructions

Bags stowage
Turret crew personal kit
NBC IPE (Incl, spare)
Webbing/ammo pouches
SA 80 magazines
Spare clothing

Right side sill
Hose assy, rubber, respirator.
Non-dedicated stowage
space for items according
to crew preference

Spare head for GNR's
sight No 9 Mk 3 (TLS)
1 x periscope AV No 40

1 x periscope AV No 40

Loader's seat
battle position

Wedge, 120mm breech opening

SHEET 6 FIGHTING COMPARTMENT, HULL AND TURNTABLE – MK 2 VEHICLES

ABOVE Challenger
**Mk 2, fighting
compartment, hull and
turntable.**

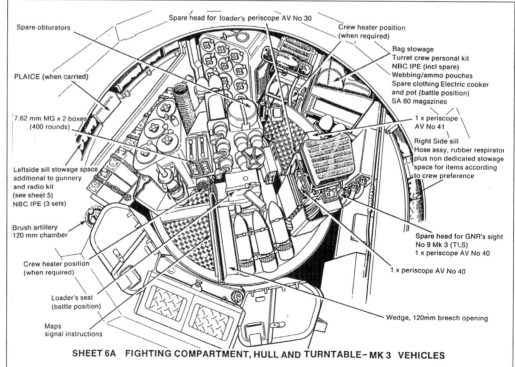

Spare head for loader's periscope AV No 30

Spare obturators

PLAICE (when carried)

7.62 mm MG x 2 boxes
(400 rounds)

Leftside sill stowage space
additional to gunnery
and radio kit
(see sheet 5)
NBC IPE (3 sets)

Brush artillery
120 mm chamber

Crew heater position
(when required)

Loader's seat
(battle position)

Maps
signal instructions

Crew heater position
(when required)

Bag stowage
Turret crew personal kit
NBC IPE (incl spare)
Webbing/ammo pouches
Spare clothing Electric cooker
and pot (battle position)
SA 80 magazines

1 x periscope
AV No 41

Right Side sill
Hose assy, rubber respirator
plus non dedicated stowage
space for items according
to crew preference

Spare head for GNR's sight
No 9 Mk 3 (TLS)
1 x periscope AV No 40

1 x periscope AV No 40

Wedge, 120mm breech opening

SHEET 6A FIGHTING COMPARTMENT, HULL AND TURNTABLE– MK 3 VEHICLES

RIGHT Challenger
**Mk 3, fighting
compartment, hull and
turntable.**

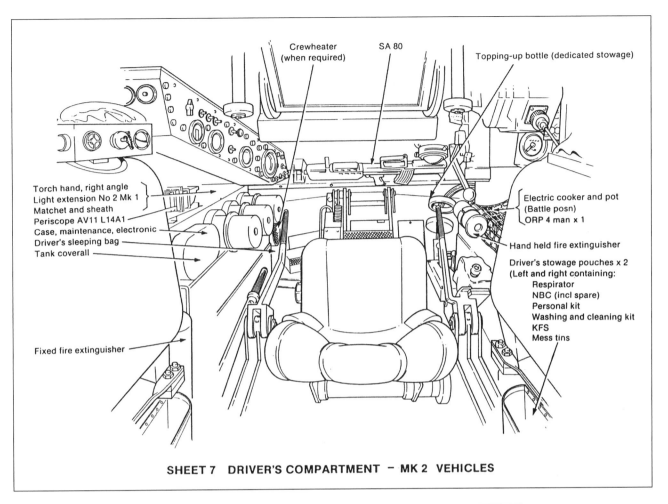

Crewheater (when required)

SA 80

Topping-up bottle (dedicated stowage)

Torch hand, right angle
Light extension No 2 Mk 1
Matchet and sheath
Periscope AV11 L14A1
Case, maintenance, electronic
Driver's sleeping bag
Tank coverall

Electric cooker and pot
(Battle posn)
ORP 4 man x 1

Hand held fire extinguisher

Driver's stowage pouches x 2
(Left and right containing:
Respirator
NBC (incl spare)
Personal kit
Washing and cleaning kit
KFS
Mess tins

Fixed fire extinguisher

SHEET 7   DRIVER'S COMPARTMENT – MK 2 VEHICLES

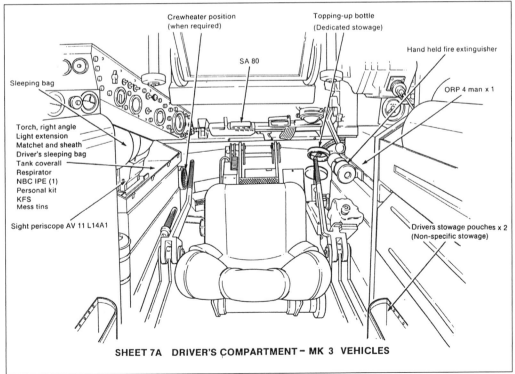

Crewheater position
(when required)

Topping-up bottle
(Dedicated stowage)

Hand held fire extinguisher

SA 80

ORP 4 man x 1

Sleeping bag

Torch, right angle
Light extension
Matchet and sheath
Driver's sleeping bag
Tank coverall
Respirator
NBC IPE (1)
Personal kit
KFS
Mess tins

Sight periscope AV 11 L14A1

Drivers stowage pouches x 2
(Non-specific stowage)

SHEET 7A DRIVER'S COMPARTMENT – MK 3 VEHICLES

ABOVE Challenger Mk 2, driver's compartment.

LEFT Challenger Mk 3, driver's compartment.

Chapter Six

Challenger 1 in service – at war and in peace

Main battle tanks of different countries are designed and built in particular ways, reflecting how an individual nation intends to fight. Arguments will always rage about which is the best tank, but it's a debate that can only be decided one way – in combat.

OPPOSITE The Gulf War. A Challenger 1 of A Sqn SCOTS DG waits by the Basra–Kuwait highway near Kuwait City following the retreat of Iraqi forces during Operation Desert Storm in 1991. *(Roger-Viollet/TopFoto)*

Production

The table below shows the production sequence for the Challengers made between the start of assembly in 1982 and when the final vehicle entered service in June 1990. Some 420 service tanks were built, 357 to equip the field regiments (four with 57 tanks, three with 43), and the remainder for trials, training, and to allow rotation through overhauls and so on. In addition, six of the seven prototypes were re-registered (but were used in the training role only).

When Challenger was first introduced TOGS was not fully ready for service. However, it was clear that as soon as the system had completed its development trials it would be included into the tank and therefore, apart from a few early tanks, Challengers left the Leeds factory in what was known as an 'oven-ready' state; that is, they were ready to be retrofitted with the TOGS system at some later date with the minimum of fuss. The presence (or absence) of the two TOGS barbettes shows which were which. The conversions were carried out by the REME, in both 18 Base Workshops in Bovington and also by 7 Armoured Workshop in Fallingbostel, Germany. Tanks without TOGS were designated

BLOCK	VRM	MARK*	QUANTITY	PRODUCTION	REMARKS
33KA	33KA91 to 99	1	9	Feb 83 to May 83	
34KA	34KA00 to 99	1	100	Jul 83 to Jan 85	06SP69 re-registered as 34KA01 1 August 1987.
35KA	35KA00 to 99	2	100	Jan 85 to Jan 86	First factory-fitted TOGS tank in this batch
36KA	36KA00 to 54	2	55	Jan 86 to Nov 86	
94KC	94KC35 to 40	Proto	6		06SP41 was not re-registered
78KF	78KF80 to 99	3	20	Dec 86 to Mar 87	
79KF	79KF00 to 59	3	60	Mar 87 to Jul 88	
64KG	64KG78 to 99	3	22	Sep 88 to Jan 89	
65KG	65KG00 to 53	3	54	Jan 89 to Jun 90	

* Almost all Mk 1s were converted to Mk 2 standard by retrofitting TOGS.

Mk 1s, even if 'oven-ready'. Tanks with TOGS fitted and the original GRP charge bins became Mk 2s, whereas a final production standard tank with armoured charge bins, a number of hull modifications and TOGS was a Mk 3.

Germany and UK

The first regiment to receive Challenger, the Royal Hussars (RH), received the last of its 57 tanks in August 1984 in Fallingbostel, and the second regiment, 2nd Royal Tank Regiment (2RTR) in the same location took over its first tank in the same month, although some deliveries were delayed because of the need to fit TOGS; 2RTR were the first unit to receive tanks fitted with the TOGS system, all the RH tanks being Mk 1s. This was followed by the equipping of the two regiments based in Munster, the 17th/21st Lancers (17/21L) starting 2 December 1985, and the Queen's Royal Irish Hussars (QRIH), from 30 May 1986. Further contracts were placed to allow a fifth, and then all seven armoured regiments based in Germany to be equipped with the new tank, allowing the Blues and Royals (RHG/D) in Sennelager (from 28 April 1987), 3RTR in

Hemer (from February 1988), and finally the Queen's Own Hussars (QOH) in Hohne (from early 1990) to be equipped.

The first complete squadron exercise of Challenger took place between October 1983 and February 1984. It was named Exercise Crimson Challenger and involved A Sqn RH. During the exercise their 14 tanks covered 21,500km, over 1,500km per tank, and thus it represented a significant test for the new tank. Prior to the exercise, the crews had completed conversion courses, with two weeks for drivers but only two days for gunners, showing how similar the turret was to Chieftain. Commanders did a one-week course, four days spent on D&M but only one on gunnery. The exercise report stated that the tanks were worked hard over different types of terrain and in a wide variety of weather conditions. It was immediately noticeable that reliability was far greater than would have been expected from a squadron of Chieftains. It went on to note that, compared with Chieftain, there was a marked increase in automotive agility, as well as better availability, in terms of both reliability and accessibility of the automotive systems, and much easier maintainability. A number of

ABOVE The crew really should have done a better job with the camouflage! The gunner's view through the TLS is obscured, and the shape of the tank has not been broken up sufficiently. *(Courtesy Andy Brend)*

ABOVE **33KA96 in the hands of the Royal Hussars (RH), fitted with the SIMFICS tactical gunnery training simulator; either the hydrogas is cold or the tracks desperately need tightening!**

problems and concerns were raised, one of which was the increased fuel consumption and therefore a reduced radius of operation when compared with Chieftain, which indicated that logistic changes would be necessary in order to support Challenger.

Although the TN37 gearbox came into the trial exercise with something of a poor reputation because of the question marks raised during the trials process, there were fewer failures than expected; seven failed during the period given an average Mean Distance Between Failures (MDBF) of just over 3,000km. Track life was estimated to be around 1,200km. Powerpack changes took about three hours

in the field, much quicker than on Chieftain, and which became even faster with familiarity. The hydrogas suspension was judged to be excellent although the squadron did pick up early indications of nitrogen leakages, which required rectification as experience was gained. It was noted that the track tensioner nuts tended to vibrate loose during road movement in a way that never happened on Chieftain; the suggestion was made that a locking device was required and in due course one was fitted, but until that was implemented it was recommended to stop every ten minutes on a road move in order to check the track tension had not been lost. The increased vibration when driving on hard surfaces was noted; in extreme circumstances it caused the cosmetic armour welds to split. It was found that rainwater was able to leak into the driver's hatch pillar and in very cold weather it then froze and caused the hatch to jam. The lack of stowage space was of particular concern, and although it was thought to be manageable for short periods when training, it was considered to be totally inadequate for sustained operations when carrying, for example, five days of rations and a full complement of ammunition – exactly the situation that was encountered in the Gulf in 1991. In general terms, though, much was learnt during the exercise and valuable lessons were passed back to those responsible for developing the tank; many improvements were made as a result.

From around 1985 onwards, Challenger became a familiar sight in Germany, taking part in Field Training Exercises (FTX); for those who were used to seeing Chieftain lumbering along at possibly 25mph on a good day, the sight of a squadron of Challengers moving down the road at speeds approaching 50mph was quite an eye-opener. For those crews who had been brought up on Chieftain many things remained the same, whilst others had to change significantly. In basic terms the tactics employed with Challenger were the

LEFT **The external fuel drums were very much part of the standard fit by 1996; the callsign of this tank is 11B, telling us that this is the commanding officer's mount.**

same as those used with Chieftain, and it was not thought necessary to massively revise the existing tactical publications. One big difference quickly identified, though, was the total inability of the infantry in their Armoured Personnel Carriers to keep up with Challenger when it was moving fast across country. The FV432 APC had struggled to stay in touch with Chieftain, and Challenger, with its 1,200bhp engine and superb hydrogas suspension system, could move across country at times twice as fast as Chieftain. The infantry could only look forward to the introduction of the Warrior Infantry Combat Vehicle in the late 1980s, but even then it was not a match for the Challenger. The increased

fuel consumption noted by the Royal Hussars did mean that there was a requirement for more and better refuelling equipment; Chieftain crews were more used to filling their tanks from jerrycans, a slow and labour-intensive process, than they were from military fuel tankers. To get the best from Challenger, additional lorry-mounted Unit Bulk Refuelling Equipments or UBREs were required to allow the crews to carry out rapid battle replenishments, which were in effect a rapid top-up of fuel – often just a two-minute 'squirt' – and then back to the battle.

In a typical year, a Germany-based Challenger-equipped armoured regiment would, as a minimum, conduct a live firing period

RIGHT Lt Dominic Carter of 3RTR in a bit of a pickle on the Hohne ranges impact area after a night march in difficult terrain; this is well beyond the scope of a troop recovery task and needs at least one CRARRV, possibly more. The red minetape is being used to denote an enemy vehicle. *(Courtesy Andy Fisher)*

LEFT The Squadron Leader of C Sqn 3RTR, Maj David Viccars, looks on whilst his loader Cpl Dave Lomax cooks the tea. The gunner and driver, Tprs Kenny Iles and Geordie Rowland look on in wonderment at the food being prepared – the umbrella by comparison seems to excite no comment.

lasting two weeks at the Hohne range complex, and also carry out a two-week tactical exercise on the Soltau training area. This would start with troop training, moving through squadron training, and probably culminate in a full regimental exercise. It was also commonplace within this fortnight to conduct a two- or three-day exercise known as troop tests, in which all the armoured troops rotated round a series of stands, both mounted and dismounted, in order to determine which was the best troop overall that year. Troop tests were fiercely contested

LEFT Exercise Iron Hammer at the end of 1988 was the first Field Training Exercise for 3RTR on Challenger and it proved to be a stern test, as every time the regiment moved east of the River Weser the temperature dropped and the snow fell – and fell – and fell. At times the exercise had to be postponed as the conditions were just too severe to allow the tanks to be driven safely on public roads.

LEFT 'Del Boy' of D Sqn RDG in Warminster. It is painted in the so-called BATUS scheme, generally used in the UK by the armoured demonstration squadron at Warminster, and has the slave lead stowage modification on the front hull. *(Courtesy Andy Brend)*

LEFT 33KA95 was one of the first Challengers fielded, originally belonging to the troop corporal of 3 Tp A Sqn RH in 1983; here it is in the UK on an exercise on Salisbury Plain with 3 Tp B Sqn 9/12L. Note the lack of bazooka plates. *(Courtesy Andy Brend)*

LEFT OB – Zero Bravo – is the callsign denoting an armoured squadron leader, a major's appointment. Unusually, this tank does not have the third antenna mounted. The crew are probably conducting a rapid withdrawal in contact, when putting the barrel over the rear decks was standard procedure to identify a withdrawing friendly tank. *(Courtesy Andy Brend)*

ABOVE Callsign 32 having a good run-out on 'the block' in Canada, 1993. The size and terrain of the Suffield training area allowed for much more realistic training than could be achieved in Germany or the UK. *(Courtesy Andy Fisher)*

and the winner was often identified by the flying of a special pennant or similar distinctive mark. But this was the minimum: in most years much more was achieved; often brigade and divisional FTXs were conducted, not on the usual small and restrictive military training areas but over the countryside of what was then West Germany. Such exercises could be a real test of the abilities of the crews to operate and maintain their tanks; the author can recall

RIGHT Until the practice was banned due to environmental considerations, the use of 'live cam' was often practised in Germany. Turfing the horizontal surfaces was a particularly effective method of camouflage, although it has not been done well on this tank. This tank also has the foam bed rolls and oil drip tray bungeed to the turret top, in a place guaranteed to obscure the commander's vision from the cupola. *(Courtesy Richard Stickland)*

one exercise period that went from two weeks on Soltau, straight into a brigade FTX of two weeks, followed immediately by a divisional FTX again of two weeks, meaning that the overall exercise period lasted a total of six weeks, all spent living in and on the tanks.

Exercises in Canada and Poland

Every other year an armoured squadron could be expected to deploy to the British Army Training Unit Suffield (BATUS) in Alberta, western Canada, to carry out a realistic and demanding three-week live Fire and Manoeuvre Exercise (FMX) on the huge prairie training area. These exercises were known as Exercise Medicine Man. Until 1993, when Challenger was deployed for the first time, one of the huge disadvantages of BATUS was that the tanks there were late mark Chieftains; regiments equipped with Challengers found it difficult to adapt to the slower and much less reliable Chieftain and in many cases had to conduct retraining for the younger crew members who had no experience of that type of tank. Indeed, by way of example, the Royal Scots Dragoon Guards (SCOTS DG) had the advantage of putting all four of the armoured squadrons through BATUS in 1990, which was in some ways excellent preparation for the deployment to the Gulf; however, much of the training value was diluted due to using an inferior vehicle. And as one of the troop leaders remarked later that year in the desert of Saudi Arabia: 'I'm really pleased that I've spent the last two years practising reserve bridge demolitions and assault river crossings!'

From 1996 the British Army in Germany were able to use the Drawsko Pomorskie training area in northern Poland for field training exercises, with the 2RTR Battlegroup being the first to train there in September 1996. The exercises came under the banner of Exercise Ulan Eagle. One of the hazards that the troops had to be aware of, was that certain parts had been used by the former Warsaw Pact forces for live chemical training, and the ground was still contaminated! But other parts of the training ground offered good and realistic training, and included old Soviet armoured vehicles and guns.

Operations Granby and Desert Shield/Sabre – the Gulf

Preparation and deployment

Rumours that the British Army might be deployed to the Gulf region after the Iraqi invasion of Kuwait in August 1990 had started to spread soon after the event, and were strengthened when the two armoured units in the 7th Armoured Brigade, the SCOTS DG and the QRIH, were asked searching – and labelled as Very Secret – questions about their equipment availability and readiness as early as 9 August 1990. Such questions ultimately derived from the political will of the Thatcher government; Alan Sharman, later to become the Challenger Project Manager, tells an interesting anecdote about the nature of the process that led to the decision to deploy.

THE THATCHER FACTOR

Alan Sharman

In 1989 the Berlin Wall came down, but before the 'do we still need tanks?' argument arose again Saddam Hussein conveniently invaded Kuwait in 1990. Challenger was to play a crucial part in the liberation of Kuwait and Prime Minister Margaret Thatcher played a key role. By then she was well aware of Challenger's limitations and called a meeting in No 10, attended by Service Chiefs, the MOD Procurement Staff and Vickers Defence Systems. She sought their collective assurances that the tank would perform reliably and to the highest standards and not prove to be an embarrassment. After much discussion she seemed to be reasonably satisfied but before they left she demanded that, individually, they were to sign and send to her, by the next day, a short paper which said, in effect, 'I, the undersigned, promise the PM that all will be well with Challenger.' She said that she would use the papers to help carry her Cabinet colleagues and in speaking to President Bush. If it all worked out the papers would be destroyed. If the tanks failed to deliver in action she would blame them! Dramatic action followed. Key spare parts were cannibalised from all the non-deploying tanks in Germany. VDS produced a number of modification kits to cope with desert deployment and sent a team to check out all the tanks in Saudi Arabia before they crossed the start line etc. As we know, there was complete success in the field, and indeed a Challenger established the world record for a tank kill at 5.1kms.

Those present at the meeting were:
- Prime Minister, Margaret Thatcher
- Defence Secretary, Tom King
- CDS, Air Marshal Sir David Craig
- CGS, Sir John Chapple
- ACDS (OR) Land, Major General Jeremy Blacker
- PM Chieftain/Challenger, Stewart Jackson*
- CEO VDS, Gerald Boxall
- PM's Adviser, Charles Powell

*It is interesting that the Procurement Executive was represented at so junior a level. Stewart Jackson was a Grade 7 (Col equivalent) civil servant.

She also told them to take 20 spare tanks above those they were proposing and, reputedly, also said that 'If you don't reach these availability and fightability targets don't look for your name in the New Year's Honours List'!

BELOW Prime Minister Margaret Thatcher riding in a RH Challenger – note the insignia on the TOGS barbette door – in 1986.

RIGHT The three main armoured regiments that fought in the Gulf War of 1991 were, from the left and in order of seniority: the Royal Scots Dragoon Guards, the Queen's Royal Irish Hussars (both in 7th Armoured Brigade), and the 14th/20th King's Hussars of 4th Armoured Brigade. Every other regiment in the Royal Armoured Corps contributed additional personnel in greater or lesser numbers to support these three units.

BELOW A 3RTR tank cannibalised for spares to support those in the Gulf. 3RTR were deployed in Northern Ireland on a six-month tour in 1990 and returned to find their Challenger fleet like this. Such Challengers were known as 'Hover Tanks'. (*Courtesy Mike Williams*)

On 14 September 1990, the official announcement was made that 7th Armoured Brigade was to deploy to Saudi Arabia on Operation Granby, allowing a hectic period of preparation for the two Challenger regiments involved. SCOTS DG had the advantage in that they were an experienced Challenger regiment, and all of the four squadrons had completed training in BATUS that year; by contrast, the QRIH had only arrived back in Germany on Challenger in April, and had originally been told that they were required to become 'Fit for War' by March 1991.

The decision was made that only the latest Challengers, Mk 3s with the Armoured Charge Bins, were to be used, precipitating a frantic exchange of tanks. As an example, the QOH were the final regiment to be issued with CR1, and thus received mostly brand new Mk 3 tanks. Stationed in Hohne, they received their first tank (64KG81) in 1989, and D Sqn was the final sub-unit to receive their 14 tanks in 1990; almost immediately they had to hand

them all over to D Sqn QRIH. In total 24 Mk 3 tanks, nearly half of the regiment, were taken off the QOH in short order and sent to the Gulf with 7th Armoured Brigade. (Later, it became clear that some Mk 2 tanks would have to be sent, and most of the 70 Mk 2s deployed were modified in theatre with the replacement ACBs, as explained in the Survivability chapter.) Forty-eight (90%) of the tanks used by SCOTS DG came from other units, including from the Life Guards (LG), who had just taken over fairly new tanks from the RHG/D. Tanks were painted, sent to the Hohne ranges for a brief but intense firing period in mid-September, and were then loaded on to ships heading for the Gulf. Once the tanks sailed on 30 September, the regiments were able to concentrate on individual skills, particularly NBC survival drills, before flying out to meet the tanks. The main part of 7th Armoured Brigade deployed by air from Germany during October, and was declared as operational after a brigade level FTX on 16 November. As soon as 7th Armoured Brigade was operational, their mileage was limited to only 15km per tank per week, partly to reduce breakdowns, but mostly to allow 4th Armoured Brigade to conduct an intensive period of work-up training on arrival. (During training in Saudi Arabia the 7th Armoured Brigade averaged around 1,000km per tank, whilst 4th Brigade, who arrived much later, still managed to average about 850km.)

When the decision was made to send a full (two-brigade) armoured division to the region, 4th Armoured Brigade deployed between 4 December 1990 and 26 January 1991, and were declared to be operational on 1 February. A single armoured regiment, the 14/20H, was

PRE-GRANBY: RAPE AND RECOVERY

Lt Col Mike Vickery, CO, 14th/20th King's Hussars (14/20H)

While 7th Armoured Brigade were preparing to depart for Operation Granby in September 1990, the Challengers (CR) of 14/20H were being stripped not only of their stocks of spares but also of parts taken from tanks in order to give them to the two tank regiments deploying, SCOTS DG and QRIH. At that time, the plan was that 4th Armoured Brigade, which included 14/20H, would not be going to Saudi Arabia until sometime in the second quarter of 1991 to take over from 7 Bde once they had been there for six months. The first complete equipments to be taken from us were all our latest Mk 3 Challengers, so we were very busy preparing those, in order that we could hand them over in top condition to their new owners. But in short order we were then required to strip our remaining tanks to provide additional spares for 7 Bde. We removed powerpacks, final drives, CIUs and the like, in a depressing series of depredations which eventually left us, by the end of October, with only one working tank. This, I insisted, remained in working order so that we could at least do some in-barracks training despite the lack of equipment. At that time manpower was also an issue: we had a reinforced squadron in Northern Ireland and a full squadron detached to Berlin (equipped with Chieftain).

In the third week of November 1990 at the Corps Commander's Conference, we received the orders that would send us to Saudi Arabia by Christmas, as the single brigade there was to be reinforced to become a two-brigade armoured division. Our first squadron had to be ready for embarkation on 9 December. At this time, although we had the manpower for three squadrons, we still had only the one tank working and a very sad-looking vehicle park full of tanks without powerpacks or final drives, and missing a multitude of smaller components which had been stripped for 7 Bde.

Replacement tanks, powerpacks, final drives, track, fire control computers, and the multitude of missing items of equipment then began to flow into the barracks at an unprecedented rate. It was clear that normal working practices and hours were not going to be enough to get us off in time. We split the regiment into work parties and shifts which worked around the clock for some six weeks. Since replacing powerpacks and final drives were both REME tasks, and we did not have enough REME to tackle all that work on their own, we used our own soldiers to do the work, overseen by REME. This certainly paid dividends later in terms of the level of knowledge and mechanical capability of our crewmen, and of the very strong bonding achieved between our crews and our quite excellent attached REME soldiers.

The first squadron was rapidly rebuilt and transported across northern Germany to the Hohne ranges, where we undertook a very painstaking Confirmation of Accuracy By Firing (CABF) – essentially a zeroing of all weaponry and all sights. We also achieved a high standard of complex gunnery tasks including conducting battle runs at night. The tanks were repainted in desert colours and were delivered to the docks just in time for departure on 9 December. It has to be said that the standard of availability and accuracy achieved by Challenger once in theatre was remarkably high, particularly considering the problems faced before deploying, the rapidity of the rebuild and the demands of gunnery preparation.

---

in the brigade, and had a number of specific problems which are explained in the accounts here written by their CO, Mike Vickery. Other issues made life difficult for the regiment. One complete troop had already been detached in September to become 4th Troop (4 Tp) in B Sqn SCOTS DG. And one of the four 14/20H squadrons was permanently detached as the Berlin armoured squadron equipped with Chieftain, so in order to bring the regiment up to full four squadron strength, A Sqn LG had to be brought in to become the fourth squadron (working as C Sqn), and had to be re-equipped to do so, as they had handed over most of their tanks to SCOTS DG in September.

In-theatre training and modifications

Some 226 Challengers (54% of the fleet) were deployed on Operation Granby. Of these, 174 were within the three armoured regiments; all were made up to Type 58 with the provision of a second tank within RHQ (callsign 22B if used by the regimental 2IC, or 11C if acting as the CO's wingman), and another two were used as the personal mounts of the two brigade commanders (callsign 14D); the remaining 50 were battle casualty replacement tanks and held within the armour replacement group. As the tanks had been designed solely for use in north-west European climatic conditions, where dust and high temperatures were not a major issue, the tanks required a series of modifications on arrival to make them better-suited to desert warfare.

The Vickers Defence Systems (VDS) and other contractor teams who deployed to Al Jubayl in Saudi Arabia were there not only to fit these 'desertisation' modifications but also to ensure that the crews fully understood the technology that they were using, particularly important as two of the three regiments had only recently converted on to Challenger and had not yet completed a full training year on the tank. The Challenger Improvement Kit or CIK fitted in the hangars comprised a total of 14 modifications, including alterations to the ME air cleaner, the powerpack and GUE cooling systems, the TOGS CSU, and fitting Sonnenschein maintenance-free batteries. C Sqn SCOTS DG also recorded that each crewman was given a VDS folding chair. The ERA (ROMOR-A) toe armour enhancement was specifically introduced when early mission analysis indicated that the Challengers would have to face a considerable threat from short-range RPGs in Kuwait City, and the VARMA (Chobham) side packs were fitted to improve protection levels for the crew from threats within the Whittaker arc. The armour packs for the tanks were ordered on 23 October 1990 (the anniversary of the Battle of El Alamein), and were fitted from February 1991. All the tanks in the armoured regiments, and two-thirds of the war maintenance reserve, were up-armoured before the ground war commenced. A number of GPS 'Trimble' packs were issued, not enough for all vehicles but sufficient for two or three per squadron, which often led to the squadron leaders having to lead their whole squadron into the advance.

Ammunition improvements derived from the ongoing CHARM 1 programme but were rushed into service – which meant that they cost a lot more than would have happened using standard procurement. In particular, under codename Jericho 2, the L26 Depleted Uranium (DU) APFSDS projectile was deployed to counter the well-protected T72M1s of the Republican Guard, and survivability was increased by bringing in a less volatile L14 bag charge to replace the L8 charge for the L23 APFSDS ammunition (Jericho 1). The cost to

the public purse of all these modifications was considerable; the table below shows the cost breakdown of the major Urgent Operational Requirements (UOR) fitted to Challenger:

MODIFICATION	MILLIONS (£)
LETHALITY	
L11 gun enhancements	0.13
120mm bag charges	10.79
CHARM 1 L26 DU APFSDS	19.84
SURVIVABILITY	
Armour side packs	9.66
Armour toe packs	3.19
MOBILITY	
Maintenance-free batteries	1.06
Post-design services and other desert modifications	2.26
TOTAL	46.93

The standard 'bomb load' to be carried was stipulated as 12 x L26 (DU) APFSDS, 20 x L23 APFSDS, 16 x HESH, and 2 x Smoke; however, post-conflict reports from the crews indicate that most tanks in 4th Armoured Brigade carried only six DU rounds, probably due to insufficient DU rounds being available in time. During the whole of the ground offensive nearly 800 L23 and over 1,000 HESH were fired in anger; no L26 was officially used as T72 was not encountered, but one tank in C Sqn SCOTS DG did fire two rounds through a berm at a T55, probably a mistake on the part of the loader. Some 54% of all engagements were against tanks, 22% against other armoured vehicles, and the remainder was against transport, infantry and area targets. Some crews chose to remove the four-round projectile rack from the turret bustle (behind the SPU) in order to mount the B radio set there to create easier access to more projectiles for the loader; one suggestion officially put forward by many crews after the war – but not actioned – was to have both radio sets mounted on the turret floor, as access to them was only routinely needed twice a day to conduct frequency changes; this would allow even more projectiles to be readily available. And because the operating position for the Boiling Vessel was in the path of recoil, meaning that it could not be used when in action, some crews lengthened the BV power leads so that they could be used whilst on the turret floor.

ABOVE The L23 APFSDS projectile on the left, with the L26 Depleted Uranium L26 on the right. *(Courtesy Nige Atkin)*

ABOVE RIGHT A SCOTS DG crewman refuelling a Challenger from a UBRE – Unit Bulk Refuelling Equipment – in Saudi Arabia … so much quicker than using jerrycans.

RIGHT How the SCOTS DG magazine viewed the official up-armouring! *(Courtesy SCOTS DG)*

I TOLD YOU HIS MOTHER WAS OVER PROTECTIVE ABOUT HIM

LEFT A Challenger fitted with the Bulldozer Earth Moving Attachment – commonly referred to as the blade. This tank probably belongs to the squadron second in command and such tanks could not be fitted with the toe armour; the blade itself offered next to nothing in the way of additional protection. *(Courtesy Dennis Lunn)*

Lt Col Mike Vickery

Our vehicles began arriving at the docks in Al Jubayl in the days before and after Christmas. They arrived in no particular order, despite careful loading lists painstakingly followed in Germany. It seemed to depend on the relative speed of the ships delivering, and in some cases whether the ship's captain preferred to spend Christmas at sea rather than in Al Jubayl. We were summoned to the quayside one morning to disembark our tanks only to find they were loaded behind a random selection of Warriors, tank transporters, 432s, trucks and recce vehicles. The captain of the ship was very insistent that they leave before Christmas, so our soldiers were asked whether they were able to drive the other vehicles off the ship. 'Of course' was the reply – no RAC soldier could resist such a challenge, and everyone from trooper, through RSM to officers, enjoyed themselves hugely driving this assorted fleet off the ship.

The tanks were driven to dockside workshops where Vickers personnel, REME and tank crews worked together to fit modifications to the Challengers. These dockside mods consisted in the main of an improved engine air filtration system with much improved sealing against dust and sand ingress, and 40 gallon fuel drums fitted on the rear of the tanks. Both these modifications proved their worth in action. We lost very few power packs due to sand ingress in the engine, compared with 7 Brigade's tanks which had not been so modified up to that time and had been used in the very dusty desert conditions prevailing in the training area. The 40 gallon fuel drums were subsequently of great use when we went through the breach unsupported by our echelon and were therefore reliant on fuel which we carried with us. They gave us an extra reach and allowed us to move fast and not have to rely on the echelon initially. An alarming side-effect of these new-look fuel drums was that some American tank soldiers told us that one of the identification features they used to recognise enemy tanks was the presence or absence of fuel drums behind the rear decks of the tank, and that our Challengers now looked to them very much like T55! Some serious AFV recognition training followed. ...

Later we were to receive further mods to be fitted by our own teams out on the training area North of Al Jubayl. The most notable of these were additional side armour packs of Chobham Armour which replaced our bazooka plates. We lined up our tanks on a flat piece of desert and several pallets of components were dropped off in front of each tank. Using printed instructions, we removed our bazooka plates and replaced them with the new armour packs. Each set of pallets came with the required tools, fixings and instructions, much like Meccano or IKEA flatpacks. It was a long day's work to up-armour the tanks, but there were no complaints as the comforting presence of Chobham armour side plates was a very popular modification. In the end, few of them were tested by incoming fire. The additional tonnage of armour did not cause any deterioration to Challenger's speed or handling, and an added bonus was that it changed the airflow round the tank in a positive way, causing less dust to be thrown up into the engine air intakes. While we were fitting the side plates, specialist teams were welding fittings on to which we bolted Explosive Reactive Armour (ERA) on the glacis plate of the tanks.

A less popular late modification was to remove the GRP charge bins in the turret of Mk 2 tanks and replace them with armoured charge bins. In order to remove the main charge bins and replace with new, armoured bins, the commander's cupola had to be removed. This was a long procedure which then necessitated a further round of sight alignment to realign the commander's sight with the gunner's sight. The bins were a different size from the original bins and had sharp corners and a different fixing on the lids. All this required time and training; the bins came in a slow stream as they were made, and we were still fitting them very close to our final deployment. Although they certainly raised the protection levels of the tanks, they proved to be very unpopular with the loaders as they were different in action from those they were used to, they obtruded into the loader's already cramped space and their sharp corners were painfully uncomfortable when the loader was thrown against them by fast driving over the uneven desert surface.

LEFT A batch of Challengers from Germany arrive at Al Jubayl in Saudi Arabia, resplendent in their new Light Stone paint, and waiting to move into the Vickers hangar so that the first of a whole series of 'desertisation' modifications could be carried out.

My second RHQ tank (I wouldn't let anyone experiment with mine) was temporarily modified by the boffins from MVEE Chobham to produce a smoke screen by spraying diesel into the exhaust outlets of the tank. This produced an alarming pillar of smoke which could be seen for miles in the desert. It prompted both my fellow cavalry commanding officers to ask me on the radio why I had brought a squadron of Chieftains out to Saudi. This potential mod was not taken up, fortunately.

The final, and certainly the most useful battle-winning modification was the fitting of Trimble/Trimpack GPS trackers to some of our vehicles. I chose to have them fitted to the two RHQ tanks, the squadron leaders' tanks, Recce troop and A1 Echelon HQ's command vehicle at first. As more became available, these were fitted to squadron 2ICs' tanks, giving squadrons the ability to split into two groups should it become necessary. GPS very soon changed our speed of advance by day and, with our TOGS, by night as well, leading to some unprecedentedly fast moves by day and night. There were other minor mods, but the major winners were the engine filtration and sealing mods, the armour packs and GPS.

BELOW The desertisation hangar in Al Jubayl.

ABOVE The Battle
of Al Kaniyeh, 25
February 1991. The
14th/20th King's
Hussars Battlegroup in
4th Armoured Brigade
assaulting objective
Copper South.
(Courtesy of the artist,
David Rowlands)

The ground war

After an intensive air campaign, the ground offensive started on 24 February 1991 – G Day. Although routinely referred to as the 'Hundred Hours War', the armoured regiments did not actually cross their start lines until the second day (G+1): they spent the first day in forward assembly areas, anxious to be given the command to move. The first tanks in 7th Armoured Brigade (from D Sqn QRIH) finally crossed their line of departure at 10:00 hours on 25 February, with 4th Armoured Brigade a couple of hours later at 19:30 hours. The British 1st Armoured Division conducted a sweeping left hook, initially north deep into Iraq and then turning east to liberate Kuwait. No Challengers were officially hit by enemy tank or anti-tank fire during the offensive, although one tank of the 14/20H was hit by 'friendly' 30mm fire from a 1st Battalion Royal Scots (1RS) Warrior into the final drive and rear hull on 27 February, but the crew were unharmed and the tank was repaired. There is also an indication that callsign 40, the troop leader of 4 Tp D Sqn SCOTS DG, was hit by a light anti-armour weapon in its side armour,

but no casualties were sustained, proving the effectiveness of the new armour packs.

No 4 Tp B Sqn QRIH led by Lt Buxton – one of the 17th/21st Lancer (17/21L) troops – reported an interesting engagement during the ground offensive: 'We advanced towards Objective Platinum 1, a regimental-sized enemy position, with our Lynx helicopters firing missiles over our heads. A vicious wind was whipping the sand up to about the level of the gunner's sight, making the visibility quite poor. Sgt Griffin in Callsign 41 observed a seething mass of men running from the position in front of him into the swirling sand. He pushed a further 200m forward, to about 1,200m short of the objective. His gunner then saw a scene straight out of Lawrence of Arabia – out of the sand clouds came three camels complete with gun-toting Arabs and soldiers on foot charging towards them. The crew burst out laughing, but because the enemy had RPGs they had to be dealt with. A short burst [of coax] was used as a warning, but 1,000 rounds later, they gave up – we think that they surrendered due to the fatigue as much as anything else!'

During the ground offensive, the Challengers in 7th Armoured Brigade covered an average of 300km per tank, whilst those on 4th Armoured Brigade just a little less at 240 per tank, as they were on the inside of the hook. The Mean Distance Between Failures (MDBF) is a method used to give an average figure of the operational life of a powerpack; on Granby this came out as 1,200km, which compares unfavourably with the GSR desire for 4,000km. However, it should be remembered that the GSR figure assumed that the tank would be operating in NW European climatic conditions, and in any case the distribution of powerpack failures was erratic: many tanks needed no changes, whereas the worst example was one tank that needed six! After the conflict, the availability (ready for combat) figures for the CR1 fleet deployed for a 13-day period including the ground offensive were recorded, and are shown in the table below:

Date	% available
20 Feb 91	94
21 Feb 91	83
22 Feb 91	98
23 Feb 91	100
24 Feb 91	100
25 Feb 91	95
26 Feb 91	93
27 Feb 91	93
28 Feb 91	93
1 Mar 91	93
2 Mar 91	95
3 Mar 91	93
4 Mar 91	98

These figures must be read with caution: high *availability* is not the same as high *reliability*. The figures achieved were certainly impressive, but came with penalties – in terms of the amount of man hours (both REME and crews) spent in maintaining and repairing the tanks, the logistic effort to move spare parts around, the effect on the remainder of the UK CR1 fleet, and of course the financial cost. Additionally, the figures do not represent the whole 24-hour period, but rather are a 'snapshot' of a specific time, and can include tanks that are not battleworthy but will be repaired within 4 hours.

Spares problems, despite the assurances given to the Prime Minister and the raping of the fleet, continued to bedevil individual tanks.

One (unknown) tank suffered a complete failure of a hydrogas unit, and went through the 100 hours with the unit removed, and so only had five roadwheel pairs on one side. Cpl Mark Collins of 14/20H fought the war with no CIU and so could not make use of the Computerised Fire Control System; it was known that a suitable spare CIU was somewhere in the logistic chain, but no one could find it in time. And callsign 12, a 17/21L-operated tank of 1 Tp C Sqn SCOTS DG fought the campaign with a petrol generator engine strapped on to the turret rear, in order to

DESERT SABRE: TOGS PROVES ITS WORTH

Lt Col Mike Vickery

Challenger was equipped with the excellent TOGS Thermal Imaging (TI) night sight. TI technology works by showing differences in temperature of less than 0.5 C as varying shades of grey. This is presented on the screen as a picture rather like a black and white TV. We were able to see 'hot spots' created by armoured vehicles at over 10kms in pitch darkness. As we approached, vehicles, trenches, equipment and people became recognisable at ranges which enabled us to shoot at them. The TOGS sight was zeroed to the main armament such that we could fire accurately in the dark. Its output was fed to the gunner and the commander of the tank.

This gave us a real technological superiority over the Iraqis, whose only night vision devices were active infra-red lights and sights. Challenger was equipped with IR detectors, so if we were illuminated by IR searchlights, we knew where they were and could engage them. Using GPS and TI together at night meant that we could move at a good speed at night, and were capable of accurate gunfire against point targets in total darkness.

There was a problem, however, as neither our supporting Warriors, nor our Recce Troop were fitted with TI. They had Image Intensifying (II) sights which depend on a certain amount of ambient light which the sight multiplies to reveal targets. Starlight is sufficient for this, but in the cloudy weather we experienced, and the fact that clouds from burning oilfields were often obscuring the stars, II was of considerably less use than TI. This difference in night vision tended to split the Challengers from the Warriors in a night attack, the very time when infantry and tanks need to work intimately together. This was further exacerbated when the infantry dismounted as they then had no night vision at all and depended on artillery, mortar and Scorpions to provide illumination for them. This light was too bright for II sights, however, causing them to white-out completely. TI is impervious to clouding over or blooming, as it is heat-dependent rather than light-dependent.

The moral of this tale is that all AFVs need to be provided with the same technology for night viewing if they are to work properly together.

CHALLENGER GUNNERY

Lt Col Mike Vickery

Challenger with its 120mm rifled gun had, by 1990, a reputation as a very effective killer, given a hit, but achieving very high accuracy at the longer ranges of the desert led to new preparation and gunnery techniques.

Just as a rifle must be zeroed, so must a tank gun. Just as rifle sights are zeroed by adjustment to the gun barrel, Challenger needed zeroing. This is a lengthy process, achieved by a procedure called Confirmation of Accuracy By Firing (CABF), in which the gun is fired at a target at exactly 1,000m and the fall of shot recorded. The system is then adjusted to take account of where the shots hit the target. Before the tactical gunnery training on Hohne ranges could begin, CABF took place, and as might be expected with the tanks being prepared for war rather than for training, the levels of accuracy were pushed to their limits by crews and REME who worked closely together to achieve these high standards.

Pre-deployment gunnery training also pushed the crews to more complex and advanced gunnery than had been seen before at Hohne. Squadrons ran night battle runs, and troop fire control training was routine. We began to see higher standards of accuracy, too, reflecting the extreme care with which CABF and fire control computer setup was undertaken.

On arrival in Al Jubayl, our tanks underwent a great deal of modification before getting out to Devil Dog Dragoon Ranges for tactical and technical gunnery training. Some of the tanks needed their CABF redoing and again, great care was taken. Our final exercise was a fire and movement battle at night where crews were learning that they could cut safety margins a good deal tighter than at Hohne or even at BATUS. Again, accuracy was honed and a higher percentage of first-round hits was seen.

When we got into action, all that training and care in preparation paid off. The first round fired by my tank was at a T55 turret showing above a berm 2,850m away. We fired Armour Piercing Fin-Stabilised Discarding Sabot (APFSDS) and hit it smack in the centre. Our crews had taken great care in the setup, which really paid dividends in the battle.

Each tank was issued with 6 APFSDS Depleted Uranium (DU) rounds, which had a bigger punch than the molybdenum-tipped ones which made up the bulk of our ammunition load. I told my crews that they should on no account fire DU at T55. It would be a waste of the ammunition which would be needed to guarantee our superiority at long range over the T72M tanks of the Republican Guard Divisions. In the end, the Republican Guard did not get in our way, so the DU rounds were not fired. High-Explosive Squash Head (HESH) was very effective against bunkers and dug-in positions and was spectacularly useful against fuel trucks. ...

power the electric GCE, which otherwise could not be operated.

It was found that the performance of the Tank Laser Sight was poor: in many cases the crews could see targets using TOGS, but the laser pulses were unable to penetrate through the obscuration that the thermal imagers could see through, so the crews had to rely on the TOGS stadiametric rangefinding system. In addition, TOGS was so good that all other British vehicles, including those with the older II sights, were at a significant disadvantage. The driver's II night periscope was poor, and commanders had to use TOGS to assist in guiding the drivers around. And just being able to detect a 'hot spot' through TOGS was not the same as being able to recognise it as a tank, and more importantly to identify it as an enemy which could then be engaged with confidence; this lack of DRI ability meant that many engagements only took place at less than 1,500m, much less than the theoretical maximum. (The search for a really reliable and foolproof Identification Friend or Foe or IFF system for tanks still goes on at the time of writing.)

Anxious not to rest on their laurels, the army conducted a series of extremely detailed investigations into the performance of the equipment used, including Challenger 1. The 'fightability' of the tank was much criticised, in particular poor ergonomics which slowed engagements down as well as causing the crews considerable discomfort – these criticisms were already well known but came into sharp focus for crews who stayed mounted for the best part of four days. Not much shooting on the move was done, only 2.4% of engagements, with most crews preferring to use the short-halt technique: acquire the target on the move, brake as hard as possible until the tank was static, rapidly engage and destroy the target and accelerate back up to speed as fast as possible.

An interesting final footnote to underline the success of Challenger in the Gulf comes from no less an authority than the Soviet military. In July and August 1991 it was reported that the Soviets had carefully studied the performance of the Coalition equipment, and concluded that Challenger was in overall terms a better battle tank than the US M1. This was due

GULF WAR TROOP SERGEANT

Sgt Tony Stirling (17/21L attached to C Sqn QRIH)

When assembling the brigade the QRIH were short of manpower and asked for volunteers. 17/21L made up the 4th troop in each squadron; in addition one troop went to SCOTS DG [as 1 Tp C Sqn]. 4 Tp C Sqn QRIH went with their own vehicles – 3 Challenger Mk 3s, and had more experience on Challenger than had the host squadron. ... This troop had very little trouble with its vehicles. Challenger is the tops for these men. The extra armour did not present too much of a problem, but access to the running gear was a pain as four [side] armour plates needed to be dropped each time.

In action the crew engaged and destroyed one T55, three MTLB and one infantry trench. ... The trench of infantry was identified by TOGS. 5 hot-spots were observed, which were the heads of infantrymen at a range of 470m. A few short bursts were fired from the coax, then a killing burst. Small arms fire was returned, so the tank fired a HESH round into the trench. This had a spectacular visual effect and was sufficient to cause the enemy to surrender.

The crews were in NBC dress state 1. The [NBC] facelet is considered to be a waste of time, and dress state 2 is not really workable in the tank. Stowage is a desperate problem. 17/21L have modified their vehicles with a Chieftain long bin and a Ferret bin on each turret ...Compo [rations] are OK, but pilchards are almost universally despised.

For observation TOGS is brilliant; it was used by day as well as by night. The coax suffered stoppages due to the [empty cartridge collection] box becoming full. ... The coax ammunition banana bin is no good as ammunition often jams. ... Spent cases from the commander's MG can jam the driver's hatch. ... The commander's seat is not liked; it is a killer on the knees. ... It is suggested that the radios could be put in the tunnel behind the [SPU]. Access to them is not too important as they are only accessed twice each day [to carry out routine frequency changes] ... each

LEFT **Crews were modified too. Here Cpl Rush (17/21L) of 4 Tp B Sqn QRIH demonstrates wearing flash hood and gloves with Combat Body Armour and an NBC suit. Crews simply could not operate with all these items on, so only NBC suits were worn.** *(Courtesy Tony Stirling)*

vehicle had a powerpack change at some time or other in theatre. ... A new air filter biscuit was fitted on the third day which made a considerable improvement in performance; the tank was doing 65kph on the final dash to the Basra road.

Overall, Challenger is well liked. It is better than Chieftain in terms of mobility and protection. It needs to be more user-friendly in terms of having fewer unnecessary knobs and switches, but it gives the crews a good sense of security and the feeling that it can do the job well.

Note: This account was taken directly from the interviews conducted with tank crews almost immediately after the ceasefire.

LEFT **The flash hood and anti-laser goggles.** *(Courtesy SCOTS DG)*

Lt Seb Pollington, 2RTR

Landing in the Gulf to prepare for war was swift and intoxicating: detached from 2RTR to command a tank troop of the 14/20H (part of the 4th Armoured Brigade commanded by Brigadier Christopher Hammerbeck, the only other officer in the Brigade with 2RTR credentials), I had only graduated from Sandhurst in April 1990. After a summer spent on the tank troop leader's course at Bovington and Lulworth, I found myself in charge of a Challenger 1 troop going into a large-scale desert war. The sense of opportunity and excitement was my overriding emotion. It was adventurous, even romantic; I felt fearless and proud. The attention of an expectant TV media world was focussed on us and we knew it. Images of Challenger 1 adorned the front pages – the tank that was the land symbol of British military might.

I enjoyed the leadership, the people and the soldiering; and my troop, which included one of the great legends of the 14/20H, Sergeant (later Lieutenant Colonel) Danny Wild, gelled quickly. The majestic main battle tank, Challenger, was ours to fight and became the reference point for my leadership. The four-man crew, and its ethos of working together at close quarters which underpinned the British approach to armoured warfare, lay at the heart of our success. We had three tanks in my troop, within a squadron of 14, and, freshly up-armoured by Vickers, they looked and felt like battle-winners.

But it was not just a lethal machine. It was also our home (almost), a sand camouflaged fortress which we painted, prepared, paraded, and planned on. The constant noise of the Rolls-Royce engines and deafening live-firing was exhilarating. So was the silence, or the whirring of just the radios inside the tank when we switched off. Especially at night; we took turns to cover the radio-stag and it epitomised the sense of team, of security in numbers, of being in it together. I used the time to write letters or plan my orders. I recall a clarity of thought and a sense of purpose about my leadership like never before (and not often since). On one occasion I was picked to brief the new Prime Minister (John Major) on the merits of the tank. He arrived in the desert on a morale boosting visit and it certainly worked for me. After the formal briefing our discussion actually centred on the ongoing 1990/91 Ashes Test series down under. He and I recalled the conversation in the committee room at the Oval years later, over a glass of wine.

During the ground war, we fought the tank in our armoured formations – and boldly. I recall multiple vehicle kills and waves of Iraqis surrendering as we advanced. The battlefield was littered with a ragged, dispirited enemy waving white flags. Occasionally rounds would fly in our direction and I dismissed the fragmentation hitting my turret. It did not matter; the sense of invincibility for a Challenger tank squadron advancing together was too powerful. And, despite the fog as we crossed the breach into Iraq (then Kuwait) at dawn – and the fog of war, which included witnessing at close quarters the terrible effects of friendly fire upon British infantrymen – we swept all aside. Firing on the move was so effective it seemed almost effortless, and the virtual-reality-style backdrop of oil installations on our (highly accurate) thermal imaging systems conveyed a video-game.

So, I lived the dream. I had my first taste of true leadership, just as Sandhurst had promised; and it was learned on Challenger 1, a vehicle which occupies such special memories.

LEFT Lt Seb Pollington of 2RTR was a young troop leader attached to the 14/20H – his short account of the war printed here makes clear the confidence that the crews had in the Challenger. (Courtesy Seb Pollington)

BELOW A huge number of Iraqi tanks, armoured personnel carriers, self-propelled guns and other vehicles were destroyed by the 120mm guns of the Challengers. Many of the vehicles had been (sensibly) abandoned by their crews prior to their destruction, but some sharp engagements took place and a number of extremely impressive first-round kills were recorded at ranges well beyond those recommended in the gunnery pamphlets.

in part to the smaller logistic 'footprint' – a way of describing the total amount of logistic support required – but also due to its fantastic levels of protection and overall survivability, the latter complemented by the adept tactical and operational handling of the tank by the crews and staff officers. A separate report on M1 noted that in dry and dusty conditions, the US tank crews had to stop after every 90 minutes' running, in order to clean out the air filters – a task which took up to an hour … hardly an act of war.

A huge number of Iraqi tanks, armoured personnel carriers, self-propelled guns and other vehicles were destroyed by the 120mm guns of the Challengers. Many of the vehicles had been (sensibly) abandoned by their crews prior to their destruction, but some sharp engagements took place and a number of extremely impressive first-round kills were recorded at ranges well beyond those recommended in the gunnery pamphlets.

ABOVE 'Churchill' was the name given to the QRIH's commanding officer's tank, a traditional name used to celebrate Winston Churchill's affiliation with one of the regiment's predecessors, the 4th Queen's Own Hussars. The callsign 11B immediately identifies the commanding officer's mount. Note that the Chobham side plates have been fitted but that the tank is still awaiting the ERA toe armour, and that the inverted recognition chevrons have not yet been painted on.

LEFT Going home. After the end of the war on 28 February the tank crews had a very short period of time to prepare the tanks for repatriation back to the UK and Germany, before they flew out to rejoin their families. The tanks were lined up in ranks with a small number of maintenance personnel responsible for them and who then loaded them on to the ships for their return. *(Courtesy Tony Stirling)*

ABOVE The IFOR badge was displayed on some but by no means all vehicles.

RIGHT 65KG17 on IFOR service in a cold Bosnian winter; the Granby armour packs were not fitted to tanks deployed in Bosnia.

Operations Resolute and Lodestar – Bosnia

No Challengers served with the United Nations Protection Force (UNPROFOR) in Bosnia–Herzegovina. However, from January 1996 on, as part of the British forces deployed under the NATO banner, a number of Challenger armoured regiments operated in the country, although generally not with their full complement of tanks, as one or more squadrons were usually mounted on Scimitars in the light role or even as infantry to conduct foot patrolling. Throughout 1996 this NATO force was known as the Implementation Force (or IFOR); the British operational name for this commitment was Operation Resolute. This commitment continued when SFOR (Stabilisation Force) took over in December 1996, becoming Operation Lodestar. Although the Challengers never had to fire in anger during these operations, the mere presence of such a potent weapon was enough to convince would-be belligerents that NATO meant business, and the deployment of a troop – or even a single tank – defused many a potential situation. Indeed, on arrival in 1996 the British conducted a firepower demonstration at the ranges at Glamoc, to an invited audience of

RIGHT A dozer tank from the QDG – note the Union flag and Welsh pennants flying from the antennas.

LEFT C Sqn QDG callsign 22 in Bosnia 1996. *(Courtesy Richard Stickland)*

ABOVE The SFOR badge; SFOR replaced IFOR after one year, from December 1996.

RIGHT A typical tank patrol through narrow streets in a Bosnian village – the view from the loader's position. *(Courtesy Richard Stickland)*

BELOW SFOR replaced IFOR; this is the King's Dragoon Guards (KDG) in the summer of either 1997 or 1999. *(Courtesy Richard Stickland)*

BELOW RIGHT No 22B leads 11B, the commanding officer's tank – both have the fluorescent orange air recognition panels bungeed to the coffin bin lid. No 11B is carrying a green plastic box in the right-hand fuel drum cradle, used as an oil drip tray in case of a leak. *(Courtesy Richard Stickland)*

military leaders from the warring factions; they went away realising that unlike the toothless UNPROFOR, IFOR had both the will and the weapons to enforce the peace.

The units that deployed to Bosnia with Challenger are listed below; in addition to the squadrons of 14 Challengers, those units which deployed with their own regimental headquarters elements also deployed the two RHQ tanks.

QRH	January to June 1996
QDG	June to December 1996
SCOTS DG	December 1996 to June 1997
B Sqn KRH	June to December 1997
A Sqn RDG	January to June 1998
B Sqn QRL	1998
B Sqn KRH	June to December 1999

Operation Agricola – Kosovo

Following the two-and-a-half-month air campaign, NATO forces entered Kosovo on 12 June 1999. Spearheading the British ground forces were the two squadrons of Challengers of the KRH Battlegroup in 4th Armoured Brigade, who, despite the obstructive efforts of the Parachute Regiment, became the first British combat unit to enter Pristina later that day. The QDG Battlegroup replaced the KRH in August, and was the second and final regiment to operate Challenger 1s in Kosovo, as they were replaced by the SCOTS DG with Challenger 2s.

LEFT It's a small world! Sgt Glen Evans, the troop sergeant of SHQ Tp D Sqn KRH, photographed by the author during the entry into Pristina. Note the usual collection of commander's items on the outside of the cupola: lumocolour map marking pens, Schermuly parachute flare, smoke grenade and so on.

Struck off strength – the end of the road

Although the surviving census records are not complete, it is possible to state with a degree of accuracy what happened to the 427 Challengers built, and which became surplus to requirement when Challenger 2 was introduced to replace the whole Challenger 1 fleet from 1998 onwards. The majority went to Jordan: 288 initially, and later another 114 Challenger tanks plus a number of Challenger driver training tanks, were gifted by the British government to Jordan to be renamed as the Al Hussein. It is presumed that 401 of these gun tanks are still in that country, as one was exchanged with the French armour museum at Saumur for a Second World War Panther tank.

The first list below shows the Challengers that are not listed as being SOS (struck off strength, aka retired) and which on the face of it appear to still be in existence. Ten of these are production vehicles. Also shown are five of the renumbered prototypes; the one prototype that was not renumbered; plus the one that went from Jordan to France; and finally, a 'funny'.

BELOW An overall view of Challenger 1 without any add-on armour. This is 34KA17 at the entrance to Stanley Barracks, Bovington, directly opposite the Tank Museum.

RIGHT **34KA18 at Borden, used as a recovery hulk.** *(Courtesy Matthew Wedgewood)*

Production

33KA92 This pre-production tank was the gate guardian at Dulmen in Germany; its present whereabouts are unknown.

34KA01 Ex-06SP69, SOS as a training aid August 2001; whereabouts unknown.

34KA11 In storage at the Tank Museum, Bovington.

34KA15 Indoor exhibit at the Defence Capability Centre, Defence Academy, Shrivenham.

34KA17 Gate guardian at Stanley Barracks, Bovington.

34KA18 SEME Bordon and used as a recovery hulk.

34KA45 SOS as a training aid August 2001; whereabouts unknown.

35KA40 This tank was listed as a training aid at 3 CS Bn REME, Barker Barracks, Paderborn, Germany.

35KA60 Gate guardian 1 (UK) Armoured Division, Herford, Germany.

64KG87 Indoor exhibit at the Tank Museum, Bovington.

Prototypes

94KC36 Indoor exhibit at the Imperial War Museum, Duxford.

94KC37 Was the outdoor exhibit at the Defence Academy, Shrivenham; sold in October 2011 and now in private hands.

94KC38 Outdoor exhibit at the Aldershot Military Museum.

94KC39 Army Foundation College, Harrogate.

94KC40 Gate guardian at Warminster.

06SP41 National Armor and Cavalry Museum, Fort Benning, Georgia (ex-Patton Museum, Fort Knox).

Funnies

66857 Le Musée des Blindés, Saumur. This is the Jordanian registration; the original number is not known.

06SP84 This was a non-armoured hull commissioned for trials work at Chertsey, where it was used with a Windsor Castle turret fitted. It is now in private hands (Mr Terry Brooks) mated to a non-armoured gun turret, and for legal reasons has the civilian plate B198AKN.

BELOW **35KA40 in a secure scrapyard in Paderborn.** *(Courtesy Dave Lomax)*

Ten Challengers are listed as being disposed of by scrapping – with the Chobham armour and other sensitive or valuable components removed, they were completely destroyed by a commercial contractor who cut them up and then melted them down. Those listed as having met this inglorious end are:

34KA28	34KA85	34KA89	34KA93
34KA97	35KA25	35KA34	35KA36
35KA50	65KG14		

In addition to these tanks, a slight mystery involves the fate of 78KF88. Its census record card notes that it was brought into service in 1987, and on 28 March 1991 was SOS as a 'Gulf casualty'. As no Challengers were hit by enemy fire during Operation Granby, it may have suffered some catastrophic non-battle damage, for example a major fire, after the campaign but before being repatriated. In either case, we can assume that it was brought back to the UK in order to remove the classified equipment before final disposal.

So in total of the 427 tanks built (420 production plus the 7 prototypes) we can account for:

- 402 tanks that went to Jordan;
- 10 service tanks that appear to be still in existence;
- 6 prototype tanks that appear to be still in existence;
- 11 written off.

Unfortunately this adds up to 429 tanks. A possible explanation is that of the four CHIP vehicles (06SP66 – 69) made, only one – 06SP69 – was subsequently renumbered with a service registration (as 34KA01), and that the other three were built with SP registrations specifically for CHIP trials and thus did not form part of the main contracts. This means that in fact 430 Challengers were built, not 427. This would further intimate that those three SP vehicles might also have been refitted to Challenger 1 production standard and included within the Jordan gift. This leaves us with three service vehicles, 33KA92, 34KA01 and 34KA45 as 'missing' tanks that definitely did not go to Jordan, and which may or may not still exist.

Chapter Seven

Modifications and variants

As well as the many thousands of modifications, large and small, that were made to Challenger throughout its lifetime to improve performance and efficiency, a number of special variants were also built. These were based on the basic tank hull design and included the Challenger Training Tank and Challenger Armoured Repair and Recovery Vehicle.

OPPOSITE CRARRV, 70KG74, was one of twelve rushed into service earlier than planned in order to support Operation Granby, where they all did sterling work and attracted much praise. This particular vehicle carried the name 'Mabel'. *(Courtesy Dennis Lunn)*

RIGHT A hit! 34KA14 demonstrates the visible effects of being knocked out using the tactical gunnery simulator SIMFICS. SIMFICS was handicapped by being a complicated system to mount and to use, with cables joining up the components and large control units inside the turret, which used up space, and so was never popular with the crews.

Introduction

Although only three marks of the tank were made, during the service life literally thousands of modifications were introduced. In the vast majority of cases, REME were responsible for carrying out these modifications and recording their embodiment. Many of the internal components on the tank bear a small metal plate known as the Mod Strike Plate; this is a simple way of keeping track of which components have been modified to which standard, as the plate bears a series of numbers, typically 1 to 20, that are struck out once the modification has been completed. It would

therefore be totally impossible to try to record all the various modifications in this book and so we shall concentrate on some of the major and more interesting ones, as well as the two main vehicle variants, the CTT and the CRARRV.

External fuel tanks

Challenger is quite a fuel-hungry tank, and despite carrying nearly 1,800 litres of usable fuel has to be refuelled at least once a day, particularly if engaged in a lot of cross-country movement. Around 1987, a number of different methods to increase the amount of fuel that Challenger could carry were being discussed. One suggestion was that the tank

BELOW A Challenger hull with the Marksman anti-aircraft turret fitted. VDS often fitted experimental systems on the hulls of a number of vehicles, and a Challenger hull was used for this purpose from 1984.

BELOW The ATDU trials of the fuel drums and mountings; due to their weight, it was a three-man task to move them from their stowage position to the upright refuelling position.

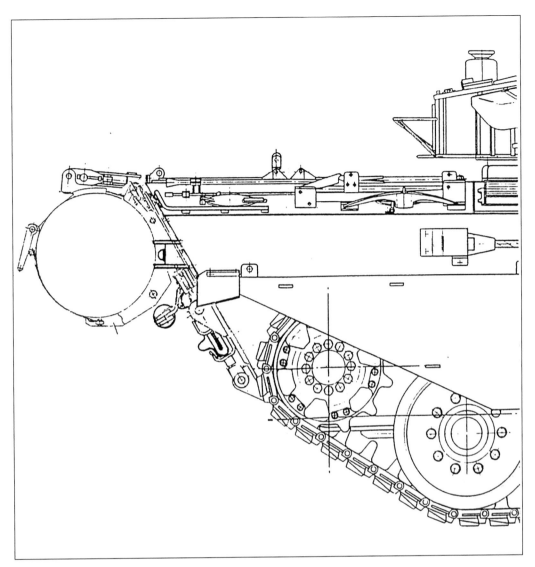

could tow a fuel trailer, but this had been tried
a number of times before including with the
Centurion tank and had never proved to be
successful, and so this idea was discarded.
Another suggestion was to mount racks of
jerrycans of diesel fuel on the rear engine
decks, and in fact the 17/21L were ordered
to try this – but not surprisingly found it to be
unworkable. The QRIH were simultaneously
tasked to conduct a trial mounting two 205-litre
fuel drums on to the rear of a tank in autumn
1987, and the first tank to be so converted
was 36KA03. This was found to be successful
and a full regimental trial by the 17/21L was
conducted on Exercise Iron Hammer in late
1988. The fuel drums required a mounting
bracket that would carry them safely whilst
also allowing the crew to easily move them into

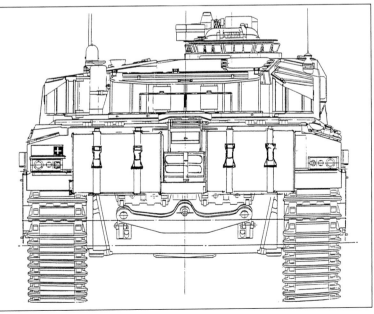

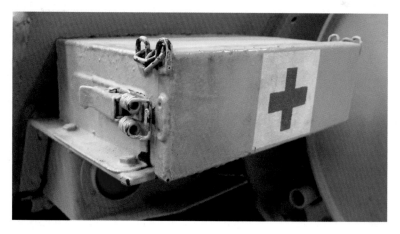

a more upright position, in order to transfer the fuel using gravity into the fuel panniers. ATDU then carried out a number of trials using tanks 34KA45, 79KF01 and also 35KA88. The experience gained from these trials led to a better understanding of the preferred method of mounting the brackets to the rear of the tanks, the relocation of tools and other components, and also alerted the designers to the fact that the drums used had to be high standard and made of heavy-gauge metal of the multi-ribbed type, and not the thinner and more flimsy domestic oil drum types. Stowage modifications associated with these fuel tanks included the relocation of the recovery equipment, the first-aid box, and two jerrycan holders mounted to

the right side of the turret to replace the two on the rear hull that were lost due to the fuel drum fitment; these jerrycans were used to carry engine and hydraulic oils etc, and not fuel. Conducting refuelling is a three-man task as each full drum weighs about 180kg, and it takes up to ten minutes to empty one drum by gravity feed into the fuel tanks. Care has to be taken when refuelling as the centre of gravity of the drums shifts during the refuelling operation and moves rearwards, so therefore the vehicle has to be level or preferably slightly nose down. Towing of the vehicle is also affected as the drums have to be raised and strapped out of the way on the engine decks, in order to allow a recovery operation to be completed.

Tank dozer

Chieftain had been able to be fitted with a dozer blade and each Chieftain squadron had one dozer-equipped tank, usually within the squadron headquarters. Despite there being (at that time) no official requirement for a dozer blade to be fitted to Challenger, in June 1987 trials began on the Pearsons Engineering Universal Dozer Kit or UDK. After initial successful trials on Chieftain, ATDU began the Challenger trial in January 1988, and

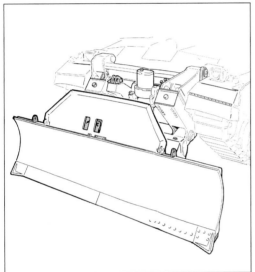

ABOVE More ATDU trials, this time of an early version of the Pearsons Engineering UDK dozer blade; note that the Challenger hull has been fitted with a reversed Chieftain 'Windsor Castle' trials turret, ballasted to bring it up to the correct weight.

LEFT The blade in the lowered position. Because the blade was not angled, it could not be used to clear surface-laid mines, as they were not pushed to the sides and away but just gathered up in front of the blade.

BELOW LEFT The dozer blade in the down position.

BELOW The simple to operate control unit with joystick, mounted in the cab above the right-hand batteries.

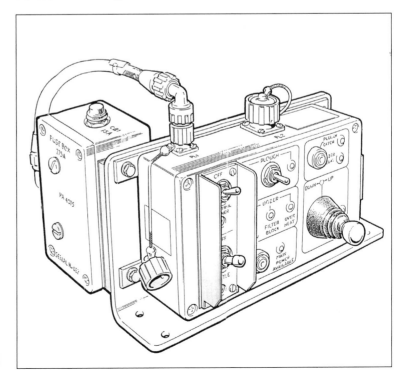

ABOVE The Pearsons Engineering Universal Dozer Kit digging a fire scrape.

LEFT The Track Width Mine Plough (TWMP) fitted to 35KA50; this only cleared a narrow lane the width of the tracks, and so was less effective than the FWMP, but had the advantage of being smaller and lighter. *(Courtesy Andy Brend)*

covered 700km using tank 34KA11. In order to mount the UDK the front of the tank had to be modified, with two anchor blocks welded on to the toe plate just below the towing bollard eyes, and a hole had to be cut through the armour in the toe plate to allow the electrical connections to be made; a circular armoured blanking plug was made to fill the hole when the dozer was not fitted. The UDK came as a self-contained kit, which included the blade, the powerpack and the necessary hydraulics; there was also an electrical

LEFT A tank scrape dug during Operation Granby. In terrain such as the desert, with little natural cover, being able to dig-in a tank into a hull-down position in ten minutes or less was a real benefit, adding to the tank's survivability – 'do not be seen, do not be hit'.

harness and, mounted in the driver's cab, the control unit. The control unit, with a joystick to control the blade, was mounted in the right side of the driver's compartment immediately above the rear of the battery housing. As the weight of the blade on the front of the tank changed the ride characteristics, the front three hydrogas units on each side had to have the nitrogen pressure increased to raise the nose and restore the normal ride. With the blade fitted the tank has to be reversed on to a tank transporter, and can only be recovered from the rear. The track tools on the glacis also have to be relocated, but the blade itself is an easy item to use and drivers can be trained to employ it effectively very quickly. The 3.78m wide blade is capable of digging a tank scrape in approximately ten minutes, allowing a tank to adopt a hull-down position in areas where there is little natural cover. When brought into service the UDK was officially referred to as the Bulldozer Earth Moving Attachment or BEMA, whilst tank crews just called it the blade or the dozer tank.

Al Hussein

In 1999 it was announced that the majority of the British Challenger 1 fleet were to be sold to Jordan. ABRO, the British Army Base Repair

LEFT A dozer tank newly converted in the Gulf – the kit was sent out and the Armoured Delivery Squadron had the task of fitting it. *(Courtesy Nige Atkin)*

Organisation, was responsible for carrying out a refurbishment programme before they could be exported and delivery could start in late 1999. Initially 288 Challengers were to be exported but this was increased by 114 more at a later date; the deal also included two Challenger Training Tanks as well as various spares and other support. In Jordanian service the King Abdullah Design and Development Bureau (KADDB) carried out a number of development activities

BELOW Unmodified Al Hussein tanks on parade in Amman, wearing the Jordanian digital camouflage.

RIGHT The much-
modified KADDB
Challenger, with
smoothbore 120mm
gun and ammunition
examples. The No
30 periscope for
the loader has been
replaced by a much
more sophisticated
affair.

including fitting the RUAG 120mm smoothbore
L/50 gun complete with autoloader. It also
had a new fire control system, commander's
panoramic sight, a new auxiliary power unit, air
conditioning, and an updated electrical system.
A further development was the completely
new Falcon turret, a low-profile turret with –
reportedly – all the crewmen located below the
turret ring.

CTT

It had long been realised that using gun tanks
to conduct driver training was unnecessarily
expensive. SR(L) 4009 issued a requirement
for the acquisition of 17 Challenger Training
Tanks or CTT; these were the first purpose-
built driver training tanks ever to be ordered for
British Army use, although the concept of such
a specialist tank was well known and had been
used by other armies on vehicles like Centurion

CENTRE AND LEFT CTT No 8 in brand-new
condition, having just come off the production
line at Barnbow, Leeds, on 20 August 1990. Note
the Unarmoured warning triangles either side
of the turret. For some reason the gun clamp
platform is fitted to this tank.

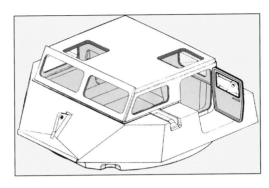

ABOVE The shell of the turret is a cast steel construction, designed to add a lot of the necessary weight back on to the CTT, but also to provide the required degree of rollover protection. The windows are made of laminated toughened glass, the two roof hatches can be used as emergency exits and the side doors have quick-release pins in place of normal hinges so that they can be jettisoned if required.

FALSE FLOOR LEVEL

ABOVE The padded and profiled commander's seat is much more comfortable than the one found on the gun tank. It can be raised on rails to give him a seated head-out position, or lowered so that he is completely within the turret. All seats have shock absorbers fitted and lap seat belts.

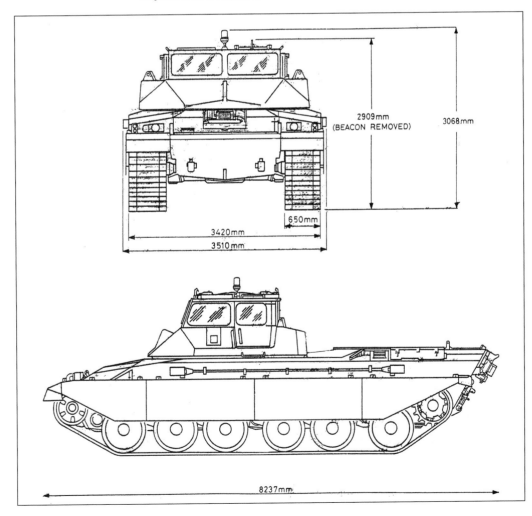

2909mm
(BEACON REMOVED)

3068mm

650mm

3420mm

3510mm

8237mm

LEFT Reproduced from an official publication, the dimensions of the CTT.

ABOVE The rollover test completed in April 1991: the tank successfully demonstrated the ability to keep the crew safe should such an accident occur.

ABOVE RIGHT AND RIGHT Two different types of the Unarmoured warning triangles: these were fitted on the outside on both sides and also inside on the 120mm gun shield of unarmoured training Challengers and the CTT fleet.

and Leopard. The CTT was based on the same hull as a Challenger 1 Mk 3 and despite not having a service turret and gun, was made up to the same weight in order to give the correct ride characteristics for the driver under training. A 'greenhouse' turret (officially called the Observation & Control Cabin) was fitted in place of the service turret, this was not armoured and was non-rotating, but made of cast steel and bolted to the upper hull. The upper roof included windows and hatches, and a basket carrying a false floor, the seats, and stowage was provided underneath. Two roof hatches were fitted along with a hinged door either side, featuring quick-release pins to allow rapid emergency exit in the case of a rollover.

CRARRV

During the initial trials by the Royal Hussars of the first full squadron of Challengers in 1983, it was realised that the Chieftain Armoured Recovery Vehicle (ARV) was unable to properly support Challenger. The Royal Ordnance Factory at Leeds was awarded a contract on 28 October 1983 to undertake a project definition study, and was able to report back just over a year later on 30 October 1984. During 1984 tenders were invited to supply such a vehicle and in June

1985 Vickers Defence Systems won the contract to provide an initial 30 vehicles. By December 1987 the first 6 development/prototype vehicles had been built at Vickers Defence Systems, Newcastle (VDS had replaced ROF as the design authority), and were under trial. In February 1989 a second contract for a further 47 vehicles was awarded to VDS, and which was followed in September that year by an order for a further 3 vehicles to take advantage of an advantageous price option within the contract. Therefore 80 vehicles were produced.

The first six unarmoured trials vehicles, coded as V1 to V6 inclusive, were delivered between August and December 1987. Almost immediately it was realised that the hull would have to be redesigned in order to make it somewhat lighter, and the first pre-production vehicle with the new hull V7 was followed by V8, the first production vehicle. The Vehicle Registration Marks (VRM) for these eight vehicles appear to have been 70KG60 to 70KG67. Vehicles 1, 2, 3, 6 and 7 were all later reworked to bring them to full production standard. After being formally accepted for service in June 1990, the first production vehicle was delivered in July 1990, the in-service date was set as May 1991, and the final production vehicle rolled out in October 1992.

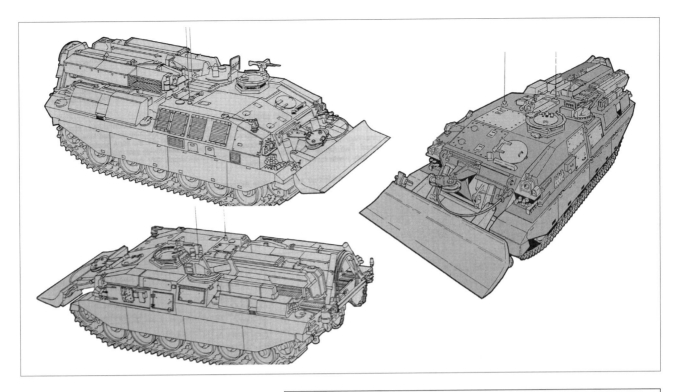

ABOVE The general layout of the CRARRV, with the Atlas crane on the right rear and the main winch unit front right.

RIGHT Another official diagram showing how the different amounts of extension and angle affected the lifting capacity. When in use for all but the lightest tasks, the dozer blade was used as the crane stabiliser.

BELOW The 'jib' or crane: the main function of this unit was for repair, in particular lifting the complete CV12 powerpack. By extending it the capacity was reduced.

BELOW RIGHT V1 prototype CRARRV – although VDS often referred to it as Rhino in their promotional literature, the name never stuck in British Army use.

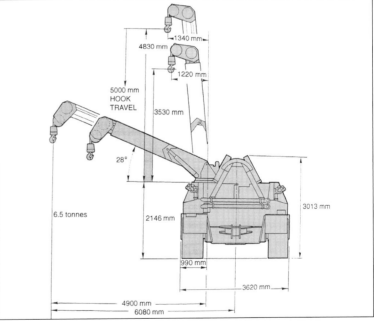

Mk 3 engine was used, but coupled to a TN54 transmission with six forward and two reverse gears. A new Digital Automotive System Control Unit or DASCU was fitted to replace both the MECU and the GCA. The Plessey APU was fitted as standard. But of course what really made the difference was the design of the various repair and recovery systems fitted to CRARRV.

In order the carry out its recovery functions a 52-ton Rotzler Treibmatic TR 2000 Winch is fitted to the front right of the hull, which carries 150m of rope. This is capable of pulling a 100-tonne deadweight over 75m by the process of multi-reeling. Immediately behind the main winch is a Plummet TL15 1.5t auxiliary winch. The crane, often referred to as the jib, is an Atlas K 6008; this can lift a 6.5-tonne

Although very much based on Challenger 1 and with the same northern European climatic conditions, CRARRV (which at one point was going to be called Rhino but the name for some reason did not stick) was able to take advantage of new technologies, particularly in the automotive area; the CV12

CRARRV ROLLOVER

By WO2 (SSM) R.J. Taylor, 2RTR

In 1995, in preparation for a deployment to BATUS in Canada, C Sqn 2RTR was training on the Hohenfels training area, a US facility in southern Germany. I was the squadron sergeant major in a Spartan light armoured vehicle, and one of my tasks was to control and account for the Squadron during certain tactical operations; one such operation was a withdrawal in contract over an Armoured Vehicle Launched Bridge. It was Standard Operating Procedure (SOP) for me to position myself very close to the bridge on the enemy bank so that I could account for the tanks as they withdrew without resorting to unnecessary radio communications, and the CRARRV would be positioned close to me in case any vehicles got into difficulties and needed recovering over the bridge.

On this particular day everything was proceeding smoothly and the time came for the CRARRV and then me to cross the bridge, leaving the last troop of three tanks on the enemy side to cover the final part of the withdrawal. Because of the danger of artillery fire when crossing obstacles, it is also SOP to close down all hatches before crossing. I lined my driver up on the bridge just behind the CRARRV, which started to drive over. When it got to the top of the bridge – and for no reason that I could discern – it suddenly crabbed over to the right, fell off the bridge on to its right-hand side, and then after a pause of a second or two, continued and rolled over until it was upside down on its roof. Immediately diesel started to spill out of the fuel tanks, although luckily the seals were doing

a good job and it was not excessive, but battery acid was also coming out and there was the danger of a fire. The trouble came in extracting the crew members: we got the first pair out fairly quickly followed by two more with a little greater difficulty. Unfortunately, extracting the driver proved to be a much more complicated task; although we did not know this at the time, the driver's footplate that his seat is mounted on to was not fixed to the hull in any way, and which in normal circumstances was not a problem. During the roll over, though, the driver had ended up being compressed in his seat but with the full weight of the floorplate bearing down on him against his hatch and was in no position to be able to extract himself despite being in great pain. The weight of him and all the metalwork made opening his hatch from outside a very difficult operation. After about, I suppose, 20 minutes we finally managed to extract him and get him into a waiting casualty evacuation helicopter to take him to hospital, although at the time it seemed very much longer.

Sometimes, it is only through unexpected accidents, incidents, or other occurrences that certain design flaws with the vehicle could be found out; no one had ever thought of the likely consequences should a CRARRV completely roll over, and therefore it was not deemed necessary to fix the driver's floorplate down in any way, as the weight of the seat and the driver would be, in normal circumstances, sufficient to keep it in place, and this had the advantage that removing it for servicing reasons would be so much easier and quicker. We live and learn.

ABOVE **70KG74, with the unofficial name 'Mabel' on the side, in Saudi Arabia, 1990.** *(Courtesy Dennis Lunn)*

ABOVE **'Barnbow Belle' on the left, alongside two previous generations of British recovery equipment, a Centurion ARV and a Chieftain ARRV.** *(Courtesy Dennis Lunn)*

weight at an extension of 4.9m, or a 5-tonne weight at 5.15m. Its main task is to conduct powerpack changes on Challenger and, as it is electrically powered, it can change its own pack. Mounted on the front of the vehicle and weighing 2.25 tonnes is a dozer blade which also acts as an earth anchor when winching and as a stabiliser when using the crane. Also carried to assist with its repair functions is a set of arc-welding equipment.

Although CRARRV was not yet officially in service, when Operation Granby was sanctioned it was clear that CRARRV would have to be sent to Saudi Arabia to support the Challengers; eventually 12 were deployed. They were:

70KG67	Charity
70KG68	Big Geordie!
70KG69	Faith
70KG70	Hope
70KG71	Moyra
70KG72	Big Alma
70KG73	Clara
70KG74	Mabel
70KG75	Florence
70KG76	Bertha
70KG79	Barnbow Belle
70KG80	Big Tyke

Faith, Hope, Charity and Big Geordie! were the first four pieces of armour to come ashore at Al Jubayl on 19 October 1990, with the first of the Challenger gun tanks following the next day. The other CRARRVs were sent to the region as soon as they were completed. The SCOTS DG Light Aid Detachment REME

recorded how effective they were: 'The most spectacular recovery job was the D Sqn sabkha site where 4 tanks, an ARRV, and a passing American M88 sank deeply into the sabkha. The only solution was a CRARRV, which made light work of it.'

ABOVE **Three of the first CRARRVs on Christmas Day 1990; note the hydrogas lean on the right-hand vehicle.** *(Courtesy Dennis Lunn)*

BELOW **This American M1A2 couldn't cope with the soft sand of Egypt in August 1992, so a British CRARRV was used to winch it out.** *(Courtesy Dennis Lunn)*

Appendix 1

Abbreviations

ABRO	Army Base Repair Organisation
ACB	Armoured Charge Bin
AH	Ampere Hour
APC	Armoured Personnel Carrier
APDS	Armour Piercing Discarding Sabot
APFSDS	Armour Piercing Fin Stabilised Discarding Sabot
APRE	Army Personnel Research Establishment
APU	Auxiliary Power Unit
ARRV	Armoured Repair and Recovery Vehicle
ARV	Armoured Recovery Vehicle
ATDU	Armour Trials and Development Unit (Bovington)
ATR	Automotive Test Rig
AV	Armoured Vehicle
BAM	Ballistic Aiming Mark (TOGS)
BATCO	Battlefield Code
BATUS	British Army Training Unit Suffield
BCF	Bromochlorodifluromethane
BEMA	Bulldozer Earth Moving Attachment
BHP	Brake Horsepower
BL	Breech Loading
BML	Breech Mechanism Lever
BOT	Breech Opening Tool
BV	Boiling Vessel
CABF	Confirmation of Accuracy by Firing
CB	Circuit Breaker
CBF	Commander's Box Fixed
CCMU	Commander's Control & Monitoring Unit (CSS)
CCU	Crew Cooling Unit
CDVU	Commander's Display and Viewer Unit (TOGS)
CE	Chemical Energy (ammunition)
CES	Complete Equipment Schedule
CFT	Commander's Functional Test
CH	Chieftain
CHARM	Chieftain/Challenger Armament Programme
CHIP	Chieftain/Challenger Improvement Programme
CIK	Challenger Improvement Kit
CIM	Classroom Instructional Mounting
CIU	Computer & Interface Unit (CSS)
CO	Commanding Officer
CPU	Commander's Pressel Unit
CSU	Coolant Supply Unit (TOGS)
CR	Challenger
CRARRV	Challenger Armoured Repair and Recovery Vehicle
CSS	Computerised Sighting System
CSU	Coolant Supply Unit (TOGS)
CTT	Challenger Training Tank
D&M	Driving and Maintenance
DGFVE	Director General Fighting Vehicles Establishment
DMU	Digital Master Unit
DPV	Directional Probability Variation
DRI	Detection, Recognition, Identification
DS/T	Discarding Sabot Tracer
ECC	Emergency Crew Control
ERA	Explosive Reactive Armour
ESR	Electro-Slag Refined
FIBUA	Fighting in Built-Up Areas
FIP	Fuel Injection Pump
FMX	Fire and Manoeuvre Exercise
FNA	Firing Needle Assembly
FTX	Field Training Exercise
FVRDE	Fighting Vehicle Research & Development Establishment
FWMP	Full Width Mine Plough
GCA	Gear Controller Automatic
GCE	Gun Control Equipment
GDVU	Gunner's Display and Viewer Unit (TOGS)
GPMG	General Purpose Machine Gun
GPS	Global Positioning System
GRP	Glass Reinforced Plastic
GSR	General Staff Requirement
GST	General Staff Target
GTS	Gunnery Training Simulator
GUE	Generating Unit Engine
HCE	Hexa Chlora Ethane
HE	High Explosive
HEAT	High Explosive Anti-Tank
HESH	High Explosive Squash Head
HET	Heavy Equipment Transporter
HF	High Frequency
HPPA	High Pressure Pure Air (TOGS)
I/C or IC	Intercommunication
ICV	Infantry Combat Vehicle

IFCS	Improved Fire Control System (Chieftain)
II	Image Intensifier
IMH	Inlet Manifold Heater
IRR	Infra-Red Reflecting
ISD	In-Service Date
KE	Kinetic Energy (ammunition)
LAD	Light Aid Detachment (REME)
LAM	Laser Aiming Mark (TOGS)
LG	Life Guards
LHS	Left Hand Side
LRU	Line Replaceable Unit
MA	Main Armament
MBS	Muzzle Bore Sight
MBSGD	Multi-Barrelled Smoke Grenade Discharger
MBT	Main Battle Tank
MDBF	Mean Distance Between Failures
ME	Main Engine
MECU	Main Engine Control Unit
MG	Machine Gun
MLI	Mid-Life Improvement
MRS	Muzzle Reference System
MV	Muzzle Velocity
MVEE	Military Vehicles and Engineering Establishment (Chertsey)
NBC	Nuclear, Biological and Chemical
NC/K	Nitro-Cellulose Kraft
NdYag	Neodymium Aluminium-Garnate
OE	Operational Emergency
OMD	Oil Mineral Detergent
PRI	Projector Reticle Image
PRV	Pressure Relief Valve
PTO	Power Take-Off
QDG	Queen's Dragoon Guards
QFC	Quadrant Fire Control
QOH	Queen's Own Hussars
QRH	Queen's Royal Hussars
QRIH	Queen's Royal Irish Hussars
QRL	Queen's Royal Lancers
RAC	Royal Armoured Corps
RACC	Royal Armoured Corps Centre (Bovington)
RARDE	Royal Armament Research and Development Establishment (Fort Halstead)
RBJ	Rotary Base Junction
RDG	Royal Dragoon Guards
REME	Royal Electrical & Mechanical Engineers

RH	Royal Hussars
RHG/D	Royal Horse Guards and 1st Dragoons (The Blues & Royals)
RHQ	Regimental Headquarters
RHS	Right Hand Side
RLC	Royal Logistic Corps
RO	Royal Ordnance PLC
ROF	Royal Ordnance Factory
RPG	Ruchnoy Protivotankovy Granatomyot, generally (but inaccurately) translated as Rocket Propelled Grenade
RTR	Royal Tank Regiment
SCOTS DG	Royal Scots Dragoon Guards
SEU	Servo Electronics Unit (TOGS)
SH/P	Squash Head Practice
SHQ	Squadron Headquarters
SOP	Standard Operating Procedure
SOS	Struck Off Strength
SPU	Symbology Processing Unit (TOGS)
SQMS	Squadron Quartermaster Sergeant
Sqn	Squadron
SR(L)	Staff Requirement (Land)
STU	Servo Trunnion Unit (TOGS)
TA	Track Adjustment
TI	Thermal Imager or Imaging
TIPU	Thermal Imaging Processing Unit (TOGS)
TISH	Thermal Imaging Sensor Head (TOGS)
TLS	Tank Laser Sight
TOGS	Thermal Observation & Gunnery Sight
Tp	Troop
TVE	Tube Vent Electric
TWMP	Track Width Mine Plough
UBRE	Unit Bulk Refuelling Equipment
UDK	Universal Dozer Kit
UOR	Urgent Operational Requirement
VDS	Vickers Defence Systems
VHF	Very High Frequency
VIRSSS	Visual & Infra-Red Smoke Screening System
VRM	Vehicle Registration Mark
VT	Vent Tube
VTL	Vent Tube Loader
WP	White Phosphorous
9/12L	9th/12th Royal Lancers
14/20H	14th/20th King's Hussars
17/21L	17th/21st Lancers

Appendix 2

Challenger 1 – technical data

Details refer to the original specification of the original Mk 1 tank; changes, modifications and upgrades are covered within the text.

NOMENCLATURE	
Designation	Tank, Combat, 120mm Gun, Challenger
NATO stock number	2350-99-893-5776
Census code	0305 3000 (Mk 1), 0305 3002 (Mk 2)

DIMENSIONS	
Length hull (front mudguard to gun crutch)	8.33m
Length gun front (muzzle to gun crutch)	11.56m
Length gun rear (front mudguard to gun muzzle in crutch)	9.80m
Height (to turret roof)	2.50m
Height (to top of commander's sight hood)	2.95m
Width (over tracks)	3.42m
Width (maximum)	3.51m
Ground clearance	0.50m
Mass (fully stowed but without crew)	62 tonnes
Crew	4
Cost (new)	c. £1.5m

CAPACITIES	
Fuel	1,797 litres maximum, 1,592 litres usable
Coolant	159 litres
ME oil	91 litres dry sump; includes 52 litres in oil reservoir
GUE oil	27 litres
Gearbox oil	85 litres
Final drive oil	4.5 litres (each)

MOBILITY	
Maximum road speed	56km/h
Maximum reverse speed	36km/h
Vertical obstacle	0.9m
Maximum gradient	58% (30°)
Trench crossing	2.8m
Fording (unprepared)	1.07m
Bridge classification	70
Ground pressure	97.7kPa (14.13lb/sq in)
Operating range (internal fuel tanks)	296km

POWERPACK

Main engine	Rolls-Royce CV12 TCA No 3 Mk 4A, 60° V12 cylinder liquid-cooled 4-stroke compression ignition diesel engine with twin turbochargers [1]
Bore	135mm
Stroke	152mm
Compression	12:1
Capacity	26.11 litres
Power	1,200bhp (895kW) @ 2,300rpm
Mass (wet)	5,488kg (complete powerpack)
Transmission	David Brown Gear Industries TN37 No 1 Mk 3 gearbox, 4 forward and 3 reverse gears
Hydraulics	Gear changing, steering, braking, lubrication
GUE	Coventry Climax H30 No 4 Mk 18H, 3-cylinder vertically opposed piston 2-stroke compression ignition diesel. Mass (wet) 410kg
Electrical system	12v negative earth insulated return system
	Four (two pairs) of 12v 100Ah lead acid hull batteries in series parallel giving 24v 200Ah. One pair of 12v 100 Ah lead acid turret (radio) batteries in series giving 24v 100Ah
	Main engine generator 28.5v 500A @ 2,300rpm and 120A @ 550/650rpm (idling)
	Generating Unit Engine generator 350A
	Lights: head, side, tail, convoy, registration plate. Trailer socket on hull rear
Fuel system:	Four fuel tanks per side sponson, each containing a resilient rubber fuel pannier; left side feeds GUE, right side ME, both via a gravity-fed base tank
Fuel consumption (road):	8 litres/km
Fuel consumption (cross-country):	13.25 litres/km
Wheels and suspension:	Rear sprocket; 6 roadwheel pairs; three top rollers (front single, centre and rear pairs); front idler/track-adjuster wheel. Each roadwheel pair mounted on the hub of a crank arm with a hydrogas suspension unit
Tracks:	650mm width, 168mm pitch cast steel single dry pin. 92 links per side (new), 87 links per side (condemnation limit). Length on ground 4.79m

LETHALITY AND SURVIVABILITY

Armament:	120mm L11A5/A7 rifled gun, firing APFSDS, APDS, HESH and Smoke ammunition. 52 rounds of ammunition. 356mils (20°) elevation, −178mils (10°) depression
	2 x 7.62mm GPMG, one mounted coaxially with the main armament, one in the commander's cupola. 4,600 rounds of ammunition.
Survivability:	Rolled Homogenous Armour welded plate frame with Chobham armour
	2 x 66mm five-barrelled smoke grenade dischargers
	No 6 Mk 2 or No 11 NBC filtration and overpressure system
	Powerpack fire warning alarm system; fixed and portable fire extinguishers

KEY DOCUMENTATION

AESP 2350-P-100-201	Operating Information
AESP 2350-P-100-522	Repair Instructions
AESP 2350-P-100-601	Maintenance Schedule
AESP 2350-P-100-701/711	Illustrated Parts List
Army Code 31410	Complete Equipment Schedule
RAC Pamphlet 48	RAC Training Volume 3 Armament

(1) Perkins Diesels acquired Rolls-Royce Diesels in 1984, taking over the Shrewsbury production facility and renaming the product.

Index